SELF-DECEPTION

STUDIES IN PHILOSOPHICAL PSYCHOLOGY

Edited by

R. F. HOLLAND

SELF-DECEPTION

by

HERBERT FINGARETTE

HUMANITIES PRESS INC
NEW YORK

Published in United States of America 1969
by Humanities Press Inc
303 Park Avenue South, New York, NY 10010

Library of Congress Catalog Card Number: 68-58415

Printed in Great Britain

TABLE OF CONTENTS

The discovery of a deceiving
principle, a lying activity
within us, can furnish an
absolutely new view of all
conscious life.

Jacques Rivière

CHAPTER ONE

INTRODUCTION

WERE a portrait of man to be drawn, one in which there would be highlighted whatever is most human, be it noble or ignoble, we should surely place well in the foreground man's enormous capacity for self-deception. The task of representing this most intimate, secret gesture would not be much easier were we to turn to what the philosophers have said. Philosophical attempts to elucidate the concept of self-deception have ended in paradox—or in loss from sight of the elusive phenomenon itself. Yet whatever is obscure about self-deception infects our understanding of what it is to be a person, what it is to know oneself, and what it is to act responsibly. Whether in morally assessing ourselves or others, whether in the court of law or in everyday life, we are beset by confusion when once we grant that the person in question is in self-deception. For as deceiver one is insincere, guilty; whereas as genuinely deceived, one is the innocent victim. What, then, shall we make of the self-deceiver, the one who is both the doer and the sufferer? Our fundamental categories are placed squarely at odds with one another.

It is easy to see that an analysis of self-deception will bear not only upon our moral assessments but also upon

1

our understanding of such concepts of perennial philosophical interest as 'know', 'intend', 'choose', and
'wish'. And the topic of self-deception also takes us
deeply into certain large-scale philosophical doctrines,
such as Sartre's and Kierkegaard's.

That we deceive ourselves as well as others was no
doubt appreciated of old, but it has become of quite
particular, explicit interest in recent centuries in the
West (cf. Peyre, Ch. 8). A Victorian such as Bulwer-
Lytton (Vol. II, p. 189) could already take it as evident
that 'The easiest person to deceive is one's own self'.
And, in mid-twentieth century, Camus, in his last
major work, *The Fall*, still could place the theme of
self-deception at the centre of his work :

. . . after prolonged research on myself, I brought out the
fundamental duplicity of the human being. Then I realized,
as a result of delving in my memory, that modesty helped
me to shine, humility to conquer, and virtue to oppress. . . .

(p. 84)

I contemplated, for instance, jostling the blind on the
street; and from the secret unexpected joy this gave me I
recognized how much a part of my soul loathed them. . . .

(p. 91)

It is of particular interest to note the remark on the
'deceiving principle within us' made by the late Jacques
Rivière, founder of the *Nouvelle Revue Française*, and
'discoverer' of Proust :

To set out upon the study of the human heart without being
informed of the existence and the activity of this principle
and without preparing oneself against its subterfuges is
like wanting to determine the nature of the depths of the
sea without a sounding instrument, by trusting the surface
of the water alone.

(p. 181)

Rivière talks of the 'deceiving principle' in the course of an essay on psychoanalysis. He expresses the early and wide-spread appreciation of the fact that one of the great regions of self-deception is the one which has been blocked out and explored by psychoanalysts. Any of an innumerable number of psychiatric case histories could serve to illustrate the point as well, but let us consider at least one briefly. It is the case of a bedridden patient in a hospital (Nemiah, pp. 126-128).

The patient was very much concerned about his disability. He insisted over and over again that he 'had to get going', that the 'inactivity was killing him', that he would 'rather be dead than a hopeless cripple'. Although he seemed to be quite sincere in making these statements, his behaviour belied his overt attitudes. During his entire stay in the hospital, he lay passively and helplessly in bed. . . .

Because his total collapse had occurred after his second operation, the focus of psychiatric interviews was directed to this event in the hope of uncovering relevant emotional problems. The patient stated in a matter-of-fact way that he had not really wanted the second operation. He had been afraid that it might make him worse; and furthermore, although he did have pain, he was satisfied with his ability to work and function despite the limitations imposed by his condition. When he was asked if he had resented the pressure brought to bear on him to undergo surgery, he denied having had such feelings. He spoke very quietly, calmly, and without show of emotions about the entire matter.

(He was given sodium amytal intravenously.) The effect of the drug was striking; as the patient now discussed the second operation, he told with considerable show of resentment how his doctors had called him almost daily to urge him to enter the hospital immediately for an operation. His family's pressure was even greater and more insistent. His mother told him 'he owed it to his family to get completely well' and that he was 'only being selfish to refuse the operation'. His wife added her urgent persuasion and finally threatened to divorce him if he did not go along with her wishes. When he finally agreed to the operation he was told that the procedure would take three hours; in actual fact, he was in the operating room for eleven hours, because 'the specialists left in the middle for lunch'. He was 'boiling mad' about this, but felt he could make no complaints because 'it might make a breach with the surgeons'. As the patient described these pressures and his attempts to withstand them, he began to express greater and greater anger at everyone involved, both family and doctors, of whom he said vehemently, 'They stink!' Suddenly, speaking of at last deciding for surgery, he said, 'So I finally decided if I had to cut my throat, I *would* cut my throat—and here I am; the family needed a lesson.'

When he awoke, (the patient) had no memory of the interview, of the rage he had expressed, or of the details of his family's and the doctors' behaviour which he had recounted while under the influence of the drug. Instead . . . he spoke without anger or feelings, and described the circumstances of his surgery exactly as he had done before being given sodium amytal.

We can be sure that an analysis of self-deception will have an intimate bearing upon such concepts as 'conscious', 'unconscious', and 'defence', and upon the elucidation of psychoanalytic and psychiatric theory more generally.

Who can doubt that we do deceive ourselves? Yet who can explain coherently and explicitly how we do so?

So long as Lucien tries only to convince others, the evil is merely embryonic; this is the first step towards hypocrisy. But have you noticed that, with Lucien, the hypocrisy becomes deeper day by day. He is the first victim of all the false motives he brings forth; eventually he convinced himself that it is these false motives that are guiding him, whereas in reality it is he who bends and guides them. The true hypocrite is the one who ceases to perceive his deception, the one who lies with sincerity.

(Gide, pp. 393-4)

'The one who lies with sincerity', who convinces himself of what he even then knows is not so, who lies to himself and to others and believes his own lie though in his heart he knows it is a lie—the phenomenon is so familiar, the task so easy, that we nod our heads and say, 'of course'. Yet, when we examine what we have said with respect to its inner coherency, we are tempted to dismiss such a description as nonsense.

In the following pages I shall try to unravel these paradoxes by getting a clear understanding of how we use the language associated with self-deception. But this way of putting matters does not adequately characterize what I am attempting to do. I am also trying to isolate, identify, and discuss certain features of the self-deception situation with which there is no everyday language associated. In order to do this, it will be necessary to bend familiar usage and develop a terminology with which we can forthrightly express certain significant, usually unexpressed features of self-deception. My aim is to develop a way of talking about self-deception which will in turn elucidate the way we usually talk about it as well as the circumstances which lead us to talk of it that way. My aim is also to develop a way of talking about self-deception which is sufficiently rooted in everyday speech so that it will amplify our everyday talk about self-deception. At present we possess a language which permits us only hints and imputations, by means of paradox; my aim is to enable us to reason explicitly and clearly about our psychological, moral, legal, or spiritual concerns insofar as self-deception is involved.

In order to develop such a language, I have avoided making out of whole cloth a new technical language (which, to a good extent, is what Freud did). I have used, instead, a family of everyday terms, metaphors and images. Speaking more broadly, I propose a non-esoteric model, an alternative to the usual models, in terms of which we can talk about such notions as 'self-deception', 'conscious', 'unconscious', and yet others to be introduced as discussion proceeds.

As the above suggests, I shall not be able to provide a complete and unequivocal set of rules for use of the terminology I do develop. Nor can there be a decisive 'proof' of the validity of my proposals. The 'argument' in favour of them lies in the plurality of profitable and interesting results which emerge from developing the approach, applying it, and relating it to other approaches to similar problems.

I attempt in Chapter Two to show why, as I see it, there has been failure in the recent efforts of philosophical analysts to provide a non-paradoxical account based on familiar models of self-deception. In doing this, my purpose is not only to present a critical review of the literature, but also to draw several general morals. One such moral is that these efforts by contemporary philosophical analysts all share a certain blindness to essential features of self-deception. Another moral we learn from the review of the analytical literature is how many are the ways of falling into this blindness. And finally, by finding ourselves forced repeatedly to re-state in a variety of contexts the central issue, we develop, I believe, a certain resistance to similar blindness when once we ourselves engage in systematic and constructive analysis.

Chapters Three and Four contain just such a systematic and constructive statement. Though there is some critical discussion of other writers, and in particular A. E. Murphy, the main effort is to give direct and substantive answers to the questions: How do we go about deceiving ourselves, Why do we deceive ourselves, What is it to be in self-deception, What are its distinctive signs, and Why are they such as they are? I aim to present the texture of our experience, not just coherently, but with the patterns more visible and their significance more clearly displayed than before. In these two chapters I am—to use a different metaphor—trying to draw a new map of the region, rather than to correct details in the familiar sort of map. I try to provide enough detail on specific check-points to make it evident that the map does correspond in its main outline with the terrain, and to warrant the hope that the new map is worth using as a basis for subsequent, more intensive explorations of particular areas within the region depicted.

The accuracy and usefulness of the new map are further confirmed in the course of the sympathetically critical exposition, in Chapters Five and Six, of other influential doctrines pertaining to self-deception and related themes, particularly those doctrines to be found in the work of Sartre, Kierkegaard, and Freud. The first part of Chapter Five consists of a systematic review of Sartre's doctrine. My aim is to show that there is a remarkable parallelism between Sartre's doctrine and my own account—with the further demonstration that, by the use of my account, translated into Sartrian terminology, Sartre's own version can be freed of much of its terminological incoherence and surface paradox. This fact has a double significance. It tends to confirm my own account, since there can hardly be any doubt that

Sartre's doctrine, whatever its defects and incoherencies, contains much that is profound and just. Moreover, this 'translatability' and parallelism also widen the scope of both my account of self-deception and of Sartre's. The fact that we can move easily from one formulation into the other means that the possibilities for mutual correction and amplification are significantly increased.

I have not attempted a similarly systematic treatment in the case of Kierkegaard. The aim of this book is essentially analytical and synthetic rather than historical or critical. I have thought it necessary to say only enough about Kierkegaard to make it plain that my own account does not have a merely coincidental parallelism to Sartre's, that my account has a generality which links it to lines of thought broadly classified today as 'Existentialist'.

In Chapter Six I have undertaken a systematic, critical re-statement of the Freudian doctrine of defence and the unconscious. I believe that the rigour and detail with which I have done this are justified by the intrinsic importance and interest of Freudian theory and, through it, of much psychiatric theory today. In addition, of course, the doctrine of Freud on defence and the unconscious also constitutes the most elaborately worked out, the most extensively applied contemporary doctrine touching self-deception. Hence I have felt, as I did in the case of Sartre, that if a convincing parallelism between my own account and Freud's could be shown, this would be very strong confirming evidence for my account. This confirmation is all the more deepened if, as is the case, my own account enables us to bring out features fundamental to Freud's doctrine which had not been appreciated before, and if it enables us to resolve, *within* the basic

Freudian framework, long-standing puzzles and inconsistencies, some long acknowledged by Freudians, some never appreciated but readily formulatable in orthodox Freudian terms.

As in the case of the discussion of Sartre, by establishing such translatability and parallelism between my own account and Freud's, the benefits of each account are available to the other. Moreover, through Freud my own account of self-deception is linked up with the great stream of contemporary psychiatric thinking, and in turn psychiatric theory is linked up with the main lines of Existentialist thought.

In the final chapter of this book, I offer a series of remarks touching upon issues which I call spiritual, and which also bear upon issues in moral theory and psychotherapeutic doctrine. I believe that much of the confusion and controversy over the moral responsibility of the self-deceiver—and the moral status of psychotherapy—can be resolved by reference to my own account of self-deception. What is more, the account of self-deception which I have given carries with it an adumbration of a doctrine concerning what it is to become and to be a person. My concluding remarks therefore deal not only with the retrogressive movement into self-deception, but also with the movement out of self-deception and into personal integrity and responsibility. These remarks thus inevitably touch upon and bring together themes already raised in earlier discussions in the book.

I have added, as an Appendix, a brief statement concerning some recent developments in certain kinds of brain surgery and the behavioural effects thereof. I place this as an appendix, and not as a portion of the main text, because the meaning of these new neuropsychological developments is still in so many ways unclear to those working in the field, and because the relation of the material to my philosophical account can be little more than speculative where it is not merely obscure. Yet what there is seems so startlingly parallel and relevant to some of the special concepts I have used in my analysis that I cannot think it should go unmentioned. What makes the parallel more striking is that the ideas of the main text were in fact worked out entirely independently of the neuropsychological material.

Faced with the choice whether or not to incorporate into the main text these essentially independent and speculative ideas concerning neuropsychology, I decided to let my own original argument and text stand entirely unchanged. But I could not resist referring the interested reader to the neuropsychological material by way of a brief summary and discussion in an appendix.

I am all too aware that much more than I have done in this book might have been done in an exploration of the enormously rich topic of self-deception. I have only one excuse for not discussing other philosophers, psychological theories, literary works, and psychological case histories: Though I have, in a way, ranged widely, my central tactical purpose has been quite circumscribed. I justify the introduction of a certain variety of materials not merely because of the intrinsic interest in each case, but because I could use the material to serve this quite specific purpose. This purpose, as I have said, is to stake out, if possible, the major landmarks for a coherent, intelligible, and large-scale conceptual map of self-deception, and to do this with just sufficient breadth of materials and detail as would show the essential accuracy of the map and the possibilities for significant further philosophical exploration which it might provide. I cannot refrain from emphasizing that, in doing this much, I have not merely written a prospectus for a map, nor have I merely sketched, as a prolegomenon, an outline of how such a map might look. I have attempted to draw the actual map, and to use it.

CHAPTER TWO

TO BELIEVE AND NOT TO BELIEVE

In recent years there has appeared in the literature of philosophical analysis a sequence of related efforts, by different authors, to clarify the use of the phrase 'self-deception' and its grammatically variant forms. The disagreements have been essentially over the detail rather than over fundamental issues—at least this is so as viewed from my own standpoint. Yet, since this group of papers represents almost the only approach to the problem reflected in the literature of philosophical analysis, it would seem that there is, generally, tacit agreement among philosophical analysts on fundamental assumptions which, if I am correct, are unjustified. As an element in my argument for a fundamental shift in approach, I propose to show that the sequence of papers in question have been—and were bound to be—inadequate even in their own terms. By examining specifically how they are internally inadequate, we see why they were fundamentally misguided in presenting the problem in those terms at all; and, seeing the problem afresh, we will be in a position in subsequent chapters to develop, in the same analytical spirit, a new way of putting the questions and, eventually, of answering them.

12

As is characteristic when paradox lies at the heart of things, there is a particular slipperiness about the object of investigation. The writers I discuss in this chapter have in each case attempted to present a non-paradoxical analysis of 'self-deception'. I aim to show that in each case there has been either or both of two results: (1) paradox has been eliminated, but what remains is no longer an account of how we actually use the term 'self-deception'; or (2) self-deception is still before us, but the paradox in the description of it, instead of being eliminated, has taken an obviously variant form.

Raphael Demos, in 1960, wrote a paper on self-deception which inspired a variety of responses. Demos first attempted to characterize self-deception in a manner faithful to the usual, paradoxical way of putting the matter. Then he attempted a non-paradoxical description of the same phenomenon. His initial characterization proceeds on the assumption that self-deception is to be understood as lying to oneself, which in turn is to be understood on the model of lying to others. Although the equivalence of deceiving others with lying to others may be questionable, since not all deception is lying, Demos' paper nevertheless serves to raise the basic issues in connection with self-deception. His assumptions are in the main intuitively plausible, though it is just such assumptions which are held by the other writers in this group to be the source of confusion and error. In my own view, however, Demos' initial and intuitively plausible formulations do constitute a sound starting point. They capture much of the essential spirit of self-deception, a spirit which quickly eludes not only the critics of Demos' thesis but also, ironically, Demos himself.

Lying to oneself, says Demos, amounts to intentionally persuading oneself to believe what one knows is not so. There is, he says, 'inner conflict' in lying to oneself; he adds that there probably exists contradiction in self-deception, and that certainly there is a paradox inherent in the very notion of lying to oneself. For the self-deceiver believes what he knows to be false; or, to put the matter more formally, the self-deceiver is blameworthy; what he does is wrong, and he knows that it is wrong. He may properly be held responsible for it (Demos, pp. 588-9).

Demos' analysis of self-deception ultimately centres on one of the variety of initial formulations he has presented: that the self-deceiver believes both p and not-p at the same time. This formula, Demos seems to think, embodies the paradox of self-deception. To remove the paradox presented by this formula is therefore to remove the paradox in the notion of self-deception. His proposed resolution of this paradox then turns on the supposition that though the self-deceiver holds two such incompatible beliefs consciously and at the same time, one of the beliefs is not 'noticed' by him. Thus (we may infer, though Demos is not explicit about this) the self-deceiver is able to retain both beliefs inasmuch as, not noticing one of them, he does not compare the two and hence does not appreciate their incompatibility.

Many questions are raised by Demos' analysis. However I am not concerned here with an exhaustive critique of Demos' discussion but with only one point: In both the initial formula ('believes both p and not-p'), and in the final solution (holding both beliefs consciously but not noticing one of them), the most distinctive elements of self-deception have been lost from sight. There is, after all, nothing deeply paradoxical about merely holding beliefs which are incompatible, i.e., beliefs in propositions which directly or in their implication contradict each other. We all no doubt have such beliefs, if only because we cannot see far enough into the implications of each of our beliefs. The child, the intellectually naïve, and the intellectually careless no doubt commonly enough hold beliefs which involve direct contradiction. If this were all that were involved in self-deception, who would be puzzled by it?

Perhaps the situation defined by Demos' final formula becomes more paradoxical if we presume, as Demos asks us to do, that the beliefs in question are both held 'consciously'. Yet the meaning here is obscure: the illustrations offered to support the thesis that both beliefs are conscious are cases where a person did '*notice*', i.e., explicitly noted, both beliefs; yet the final solution supposes that in self-deception both beliefs are conscious but one is *not* noticed (p. 591).

The central difficulty with Demos' formulation, however, does not lie in the obscurity of meaning of 'conscious', 'notice', and 'attend' as Demos uses these. It lies in the failure to distinguish between commonplace inconsistency in beliefs on the one hand, and self-deception on the other. This distinction would require, at least as a beginning, a clear answer from Demos to the crucial question: Is the 'not noticing' or 'not attending' to the belief intentional? Are we to suppose that the person does not notice one belief because he knows that there is an inconsistency, and wishing not to notice this inconsistency, he avoids noticing the belief? Or does he just happen not to notice the belief or the inconsistency? The latter is commonplace ignorance; the former is self-deception —and it is as paradoxical in its formulation as ever. Such questions, however, are not clearly answered, indeed they are not even explicitly raised by Demos. Nevertheless it will be of some interest to follow how this issue raises itself, tacitly, as Demos tries variant phrasings in which to express his view.

Demos is led to say that the self-deceiver 'fails to notice', (p. 594), is 'distracted from' (p. 593) the belief; but if this is so, the essential purposefulness is absent. This may be oversight or confusion, but it is neither self-deception nor is it 'blameworthy' as such. On the other hand, when Demos says—without remarking the difference—that the self-deceiver 'deliberately ignores' (p. 593) the belief, we are once again faced with genuine self-deception—but also with paradox. For now it appears that it is just because he *already* appreciates the incompatibility of his beliefs that the self-deceiver 'deliberately ignores' the belief he abhors.

It is a natural enough proposal, having come to a dead end, that we consider whether or not the initial assumption of Demos may not be the source of difficulty. Siegler in effect proposes, reasonably enough, that merely because we use the word 'deception' in 'self-deception', we need not feel required to suppose that it is used in much the same way as it is when we speak of deceiving other persons. It may be, he argues, that the use of 'self-deception', or, more generally, the use of 'reflexive deception expressions', has other 'functions' than to report or ascribe or express something closely akin to lying or even to the concurrent holding of conflicting beliefs (pp. 473ff.).

Siegler offers, presumably as a particular form of what we could call self-deception, a number of examples based on the kind of situation where a person finally declares, perhaps after failing an examination or getting nowhere with women, 'I knew all along . . .' (e.g., that I would fail, or, that I would get nowhere). The person's later declaration contrasts with his having earlier acted the ladies' man or the sure success. Siegler's specific proposals begin with the clearly innocuous thesis, related to his main thesis, that merely because a person *says* 'I knew all along . . .' we need not suppose that he did in fact know.

Siegler then offers a lengthy sequence of proposals as to how 'reflexive deception expressions' really do 'function'. In each proposal, his aim is to eliminate the necessity to suppose concurrent conflicting beliefs. In this, his general strategy is of course explicitly opposed to Demos'. For the sake of brevity, I have organized Siegler's proposals into groups, and I present my own comment briefly in each case.

(1) Saying 'I knew all along . . .' may be intended to serve as pretence to others. *Comment*: this is true; however insofar as it is simply this, we could not call this self-deception, but merely an attempt to deceive others. See further comment under (2).

(2) Saying 'I knew all along . . .' may serve as an attempt to discount or minimize one's failure in some effort. Presumably Siegler's point here is that the person claims that although he let it appear he thought he would succeed, he himself was fully aware of the truth all along. *Comment*: This raises many questions. Is the minimizing of the failure bona fide? Was it truly the case that the person was pretending to others but appeared in his true light to himself? Then his claim to have been prescient is sound, and there is no reason to consider this a case of self-deception. Or was he—as Siegler says without further comment at one point—'taken in by his own pretences'? If the latter is the case, we may have a case of self-deception, but

Siegler's analysis throws no light on how one can take oneself in by one's own pretences.

Siegler's remarks are also unclear as to whether he takes 'I knew all along . . .' to express *past* self-deception, or whether the person is supposed to be in the act of deceiving himself *now*. If the latter be the case, the question we must ask is: In saying 'I knew all along . . .' does the man now honestly think this to be true, though in fact it is not? Or does he say this as an element in trying to persuade himself now—and with some success—that it's true, even though he knows that it is false? If it is the former case, it is not self-deception now, though it may be poor memory, or some other kind of error or confusion. If the latter is the case, then he is now deceiving himself, but the description is paradoxical. Yet the two types of case are surely distinguishable.

(3) Saying 'I knew all along . . .' is simply a reference to past fears, or hopes, or apprehensions, rather than to knowledge. For example, the man did *fear* he would fail, and having failed he now says that he *knew* all along he would fail. *Comment*: Then the statement 'I knew all along . . .' is false. The speaker is careless, or his memory is at fault, or he is confused. However this case, too, could be interpreted as an attempt to deceive himself *now*: we might assume that the speaker has in a way now persuaded himself to believe that he 'knew all along' in order to hide from himself the known and unpalatable truth that he did not actually know all along but only feared. But if we interpret the case in this way, we have had to reintroduce the paradox of a person persuading himself to believe what he knows isn't so.

(4) A mother who *says* she does not believe that her son is a scoundrel, in spite of overwhelming evidence

to this effect, may in this way be expressing not disbelief but her inability to understand how her son could be a scoundrel. *Comment*: This is not necessarily a case of self-deception. There is an identifiable difference between a woman who cannot understand how her son could be a scoundrel—however inaccurately she expresses this—and a woman who, whether or not she understands how it could be, knows that in any case it *is* so. The former is perplexed, but not in self-deception. The latter woman need not be in self-deception; however she may find the fact so painful to contemplate that she tries, with some success, to make it appear to herself that it is not so. She is *then* deceiving herself, and again the characterization is paradoxical.

(5) The mother's self-deception, says Siegler, may consist in her claiming to believe her son is a fine boy because she *wants* so much that this should be so. *Comment*: Again, the case as described need not be self-deception. The crucial question is whether she not only wants it to be true that he's a good boy, but also has persuaded herself to *believe* it. 'Wishful thinking' is not merely saying that one believes something to be so, not merely wanting it to be so, but in some way believing it to be so. There is often no practical difficulty in distinguishing these three different possibilities from one another. Each of us has biasses which affect the formation of his beliefs and attitudes without his knowing or intending that they should. If having a passionate wish that something should be so brings it about unintentionally that one believes it so, this may with some propriety be called self-deception, though I believe we are much more likely to call it prejudice or wishful thinking. To the extent that we suppose the belief to be intentionally cultivated because of the wish to be-

lieve, we distinguish the case as one of self-deception, a less innocent and philosophically far more interesting kind of wishful thinking. We suspect the latter type more readily in the case of the mother with an obviously scoundrelly son, whereas we usually suppose that it is the more innocent type of wishful thinking when we notice, in less dramatic circumstances, that a mother merely has a somewhat more favourable view of her son than does the disinterested observer. The more innocent form of wishful thinking shades into the most flagrant form of self-deception. When I speak of self-deception, I shall not mean to include the 'innocent kind', i.e., the cases where the belief is not induced purposely and with knowledge that it is false.

(6) Saying 'I knew all along . . .' serves, says Siegler, as the expression of a *new* insight on the basis of memory. *Comment*: This is not self-deception. 'I knew all along . . .' if used this way, is a misleading way of saying 'I *now* for the first time see what I could have seen before had I only looked at things in the right way.' We would not call this a case of self-deception—unless we further supposed that the reason I didn't 'look' was because I knew very well I wouldn't like what I'd see, and so I kept my eyes averted. But then we are back with the paradoxical form of self-deception: somehow managing to pretend to myself that there's nothing there to be seen, just because I know very well that there is something unbearably distressing to be seen.

(7) 'I have been deceiving myself . . .' may merely express, according to Siegler, a resolve to change, or a spur to such resolve; or it may serve as a warning to oneself, an accusation, a reprimand, advice to reconsider. *Comment:* Of course this phrase might serve for these purposes—but so might any of a number of

others which are not 'reflexive deception expressions', for example: 'I've been lazy,' 'I've been thoughtless,' 'I've been insensitive,' 'I've been a glutton.' Though any of these may serve as spurs to change, as self-accusations, and so on, we do not use them indiscriminately as equivalents of one another. What is essential to our purpose, and what Siegler does not give us, is knowledge of the conditions which warrant reprimanding oneself specifically as a self-deceiver rather than, perhaps, a glutton.

(8) The remaining proposals by Siegler are closely akin to the proposal which is central to a paper by Canfield and Gustafson. In Siegler's case, the suggestion is that the ascription of self-deception to oneself may merely be the expression of one's judgment that one should have known better but didn't. Siegler also gives a somewhat different version of this proposal: to ascribe self-deception to someone is to attribute to him an erroneous belief which it is unreasonable to have, and to ascribe responsibility to him for this. Let us postpone comment on this last proposal until we have briefly reviewed the form in which Canfield and Gustafson (hereafter 'C-G') present it.

C-G, like Siegler, are critical of the fundamental assumption of writers like Demos (and, as they point out, Sartre too) that the 'deception' in 'self-deception' is to be understood very much as it is when we speak of one person deceiving another. They present an argument intended to treat self-deception as a species of 'self-command', and to show, in turn, that the 'logic' of 'self-command' is different from that of 'other-command' and is quite non-paradoxical. In the course of their argument, C-G treat 'making oneself do something', 'telling oneself to do something', and 'requesting oneself to do something' as interchangeable with 'self-command'. Then, focussing upon 'making oneself do something' they hold that this comes to 'doing something in adverse circumstances'. Self-deception is then announced to be 'making oneself believe (or forget) something'.

This elaborate argument rests on the unwarranted interchanging of a number of idioms which are quite different in their sense, and on erroneous analyses of such phrases as 'make oneself do something'. Nevertheless C-G's conclusion, whatever the failings of their argument, deserves to be examined on its intrinsic merits since it is essentially the same as suggested by Siegler, and it is also, as we shall see, accepted and elaborated further by Penelhum. Their conclusion is: 'All that happens in self-deception, we suggest, is that the person believes or forgets something in [belief-adverse] circumstances' (i.e., in circumstances which point overwhelmingly to the conclusion opposite to the one adopted by the self-deceiver) (C-G, 35). As will be recalled, this is very much like Siegler's formulae, 'erroneous belief which it is unreasonable to have', and, 'one should have known better'. We must now ask whether any such formulae can encompass our everyday use of 'self-deception'.

Let us begin by supposing that in a particular instance the circumstances, evidence, or argument favouring a certain belief are presented to Jones, who holds the contrary belief. The argument, however, is so complex or esoteric that only an expert—which Jones is not—could appreciate how overwhelmingly it points to a certain conclusion. Jones does not grasp the force of the evidence, and he maintains his former belief. In this instance, which appears to satisfy the conditions set down by C-G for self-deception, we would not normally say that Jones is self-deceived. Let us suppose another instance. Although expertise is not required, Smith happens to be quite dull, or emotionally upset and distracted, and he does not appreciate what a layman of average intelligence, with his wits about him, would appreciate. Smith would still, perhaps, believe contrary to strong evidence, but he would not be a self-deceiver. Further we may suppose a person who is thoughtless, or impulsive, or intellectually lazy, careless, or confused, or simply stupidly stubborn. Such a person might well believe contrary to strong evidence, or, in Siegler's terms, hold an 'erroneous belief which it is unreasonable to hold' and about which he 'should have known better'. Yet we would not consider this in itself to be self-deception.

It may be, however, that the idea of believing something in the face of belief-adverse circumstances was all along meant to include the idea that the person knows and *appreciates* the force of the belief-adverse circumstances or the evidence. This issue is never raised by C-G or by Siegler, but it is pressed vigorously by Penelhum.

Penelhum begins by agreeing that Demos' original assumption—that self-deception is to be understood on the model of 'other-deception'—is the wrong way to go about the matter; and he also agrees with Canfield and Gustafson that belief in the face of strong evidence is a necessary condition of self-deception, but he argues that it is not a sufficient condition. Penelhum stresses that not only must the evidence against the belief be strong, but it is essential that the person know the evidence, and moreover the person must see the import of what he knows. If all these conditions are satisfied, says Penelhum, this amounts to his accepting the conclusion to which the evidence points: 'for the criteria for saying that he really does see where the evidence points and the criteria for saying that he accepts the conclusion are the same'.

To avoid reinstating what he takes to be typical paradoxical renderings of self-deception, Penelhum further proposes what amounts to an interesting variant of one of Demos' theses. Penelhum postulates that self-deception is a 'conflict state': 'Someone in this state does partially satisfy the criteria for belief and also those for disbelief—in particular he will tend to declare his disbelief in that to which he sees the evidence points' (pp. 258-9).

This latter proposal can be helpful, but it is vague as presented, and it is radically incomplete even if one accepts the spirit of the approach. What is meant by 'partially satisfy the criteria of belief'? And why not require that the criteria of belief be wholly satisfied? Penelhum himself states that the mere tendency to declare disbelief is not enough; 'there must be some reason to say that he does believe what he asserts' when he asserts his disbelief. What would such a reason be? Would any sort of reason do? Or are there certain types of reasons which are characteristically available in the case of self-deception, others being characteristically absent? Since the reasons which count heavily for supposing a person believes what he asserts usually vary with context, we might suppose that much of our insight into self-deception will come from specifying what there is about the person's comportment, in addition to his *saying* that he believes something, that leads us to put trust in what he says. If we think a person who says he holds a certain belief is joking with us, then we may ask him if he is; and if he replies that he is not, then this is typically a good reason to think that he said what he believed. But this particular question and answer would give little reason to suppose the person was not deceiving himself. If we suspected he was in self-deception, a negative answer to our asking whether he is deceiving himself would not settle the issue at all.

Perhaps it is helpful to shift the analysis of 'self-deception', as Penelhum does, from the question whether a person both believes and disbelieves, to the question as to what reasons we have for saying the self-deceiver believes and what reasons for saying he disbelieves. But to leave the question there, as Penelhum seems to do, is to hint at a method of analysis rather than to carry the analysis through.

Matters are unhappily returned to deeper obscurity when Penelhum proceeds (p. 259) to a more formal statement of 'the necessary and jointly sufficient criteria for self-deception (over matters other than one's own inner stages)'. These criteria, he says, are:
  (1) belief in the face of strong evidence,
  (2) the subject's knowledge of the evidence,
  (3) the subject's recognition of the import of the evidence.

This formal statement confuses matters because in (1) it replaces the earlier expository phrase, 'partially satisfy the criteria for belief', with the simple word 'belief', and in (2) and (3) we have what according to Penelhum's earlier comments are the jointly sufficient criteria for saying that the subject has accepted the counter-belief. Thus what we now have is, in effect, the thesis that self-deception consists in believing what strong evidence shows to be so (by virtue of 2 and 3), and at the same time believing to the contrary (by virtue of 1). This reinstates, in slightly indirect language, the very situation which Penelhum was concerned to avoid.

Once again, we see that the problem has been defined in substantially the terms favoured by Demos—the co-existence in one person of two incompatible beliefs. Whether these are, as it were, 'half-beliefs', or whether one or both are irrational, does not change matters fundamentally.

Let us attempt a strict application of Penelhum's formula, which is, after all, the most refined version of an approach basically favoured by the entire group of writers we have considered. Suppose we come across a person with a tendency to declare a certain belief and to show other persuasive signs of genuinely believing; furthermore he knows the decisive evidence against this belief, and he appreciates its import. Suppose now that we were to ask such a person if he believed the conclusion to which he appreciates that the strong evidence points; and suppose he were to reply that he does believe the conclusion to which that evidence points, but that he continues to believe the contrary as well. What would we say then? We would surely be puzzled. We might charge him with indecisiveness. He assures us he believes, not half-believes. We remain puzzled. Yet we would not say that he is evidently a self-deceiver. Perhaps he's confused, or out of his mind, or doesn't understand the language well. Perhaps he's something of a 'divided personality'. It is not for us to struggle with this case further but to see that the present difficulty arises because he acknowledges holding the belief which is consistent with the evidence. Yet, according to Penelhum's three criteria of self-deception, this man is a self-deceiver.

Clearly, Penelhum has omitted from his formula a

further condition, namely, that the person who appreciates the import of the strong evidence nevertheless
denies, with some evidence of sincerity, that he believes
what we somehow know him to see the evidence
proves. Or if he does not explicitly deny the belief, he
must give the convincing impression that he would,
given appropriate occasion, not only deny it but do so
with a certain sincerity.

I think it is also required that he deny, with a certain
sincerity, not only the belief, but even that he sees the
way the evidence points (though by the hypothesis he
does see this). For, even were he to confess seeing
where the evidence points and that it is decisive, and
were he nevertheless to deny with a certain sincerity
that he believes the conclusion to which it points, we
would not necessarily consider him in self-deception.
Such a case might merely present a puzzle to us. Or it
could be the kind of case where a mother suddenly, but
with complete and obvious reliability, is informed that
her child has been killed. It takes her a while to absorb
the shocking news—'She knows it's true, yet can't believe it.' That is, she sees where the evidence points,
but is too shocked to have responded with her own
affirmative belief. This could shade into self-deception
with time. What would lead us towards the latter characterization would be the growing belief on our part
that the truth is beginning to 'seep in', that having be-
gun to assimilate the truth, she is now fighting, with
a certain success, to deny the import of the evidence
or its decisiveness; in short, she is trying to keep herself
persuaded that what she knows in her heart to be true
is really not true. Thus the self-deceiver must, with a
certain sincerity, not only deny believing but also deny
seeing that the conclusion is established by the evidence.

The modification of Penelhum's formula to include

denial of the belief to which the evidence points, and denial that the evidence is seen to point decisively to that conclusion, still omits the crucial element of purposefulness in the whole manoeuvre. A person is not a self-deceiver if, as a result of instructions by a hypnotist, he affirms a belief with a certain sincerity and also denies, with a certain sincerity, that he sees the patently decisive evidence to the contrary to be decisive. Nor is he a self-deceiver if such comportment is the outcome of strictly neurological malfunction. He must not be merely intellectually indecisive or defective, or subject to such strong and stubborn habits that he acts in this inconsistent way because of long and firm commitment to a belief which is refuted by evidence which, perhaps, is just now and for the first time before him. The crucial element which is necessary—and which would exclude all these possibilities—is the element of purposefulness. If our subject *persuades* himself to believe contrary to the evidence *in order to evade*, somehow, the unpleasant truth to which he has already seen that the evidence points, then and only then is he clearly a self-deceiver.

Penelhum is no doubt the more susceptible to overlooking the element of purposefulness because he has correctly seen that *motive* is not of the essence of self-deception, though it is in practice an important factor in self-deception. Penelhum does not distinguish in his discussion between what we may call motive and purpose. It is correct to say that, even if we assume no motive, we would call a person self-deceived if he persuaded himself to believe what in his heart he knows is not so. Normally we assume a motive for doing this; in most general terms we usually assume the person is moved to self-deception as a way of attempting to evade distress, or as a way of attempting to maximize satisfaction. Penelhum says, with a certain justice, that this is a question likely to be more of a psychological kind than a conceptual kind. What Penelhum does not see is that, whatever the motive for engaging in self-deception, or whether there be any motive at all, self-deception necessarily contains within itself, as we have seen, a certain purposefulness. This element of internal purposefulness is reflected in such phrases as 'persuades himself to believe', 'makes it appear to himself', 'lies to himself'. It is what is lacking, for example, in the case of the person who carries on much like the self-deceiver but does so by virtue of hypnotic command.

Up to this point I have concentrated on trying to show that, in their anxiety to resolve the supposed paradox in maintaining that a person holds two incompatible beliefs, Demos, Siegler, Canfield and Gustafson, and Penelhum all fail to appreciate that the deep paradox of self-deception lies not in this at most mildly odd condition, but in the element of knowing, intentional ignorance. Another important theme is to be found in their proposals, however, and it deserves comment. It is to the effect that the belief affirmed explicitly by a self-deceiver is contrary to the evidence. I propose to dwell briefly on this second theme in order to show that belief in the face of contrary evidence is not a necessary condition of self-deception. (That it is not a sufficient condition has been shown by my earlier examples of persons who hold such beliefs but are not in self-deception.)

Imagine a person who jumps hastily to conclusions, whose beliefs and attitudes are formed not by careful attention to evidence but by bias, inclination, and sloppy thinking—a not uncommon type. Imagine further that, on the basis of fear and as an outcome of intellectual fuzziness, this person jumps to the conclusion that he has cancer. The evidence is not strong, but his belief is. It is not even that he thinks he has received evidence or argument; he is confessedly the 'intuitive' type: He 'just knows' he has cancer. This belief causes him unbearable distress. In order to ameliorate his distress, he proceeds to try now to re-assure himself, to persuade himself that he does not have cancer, that he's 'the picture of health'. The twinge which, in his heart, he 'knows' to be the symptom of cancer, he half-convinces himself is 'just a twinge'. We who observe him say: 'Deep down in his heart he's scared stiff of dying; he just knows he has cancer. But on the surface, that elaborate air of equanimity, of supreme confidence is an attempt to reassure himself. And in a way he's taken in by it himself.'

What counts in this case is not the strength of the evidence that he has cancer but the strength of his original and unshakeable belief that he does. It is by no means rare, indeed it is common, for individuals to arrive at deeply held, distressing beliefs on the basis of inadequate evidence—and it is not so rare that the person attempts then to persuade himself that what he takes to be so isn't really so. Here the self-deception is rooted in the opposition between the declared belief and the denied belief, not in the relation of either belief to the evidence.

The 'two-belief' approach as a non-paradoxical basis for elucidating the meaning of self-deception allows of several variants not yet considered. Since they have an initial plausibility, they merit brief review. This group of proposals rests on the assumption that the incompatible beliefs are not held at the very same time.

The person who shifts from one belief to the opposing belief may merely be indecisive or he may have changed his mind for good reason. Perhaps, however, the person wishes to believe other than he does; he so arranges matters that he is subject to influences, over a period of time, which eventually lead him in fact to believe what he had originally disbelieved but had wanted to believe. Of course, for this to be plausible as an example of self-deception specifically, the influences must be such that he welcomes them even though he recognizes their inadequacy for *warranting* his change of belief. Thus, a person previously objective in evaluating his capacities, now weary of life's strain takes to drinking heavily. He knows this will initially dull his sensibilities, eventually permanently undermine his capacities for self-evaluation. He does not care, indeed he cynically welcomes the expected respite. He knows he will mingle more and more with people who tell him what he would like to hear, and that less and less will he have the capacity to see through this. Even in such a case, I do not think we would say that such a person deceived himself. He has knowingly put himself in a position where he can *be* deceived, but he is not deceiving himself.

A different type of case in which one belief induces a later, incompatible belief is that of the over-ingenious swindler. He has laid out such a complicated and nefarious maze to confuse his victims that finally he himself is tangled in his own web. We might say that he has deceived himself. Yet evidently this is quite a different thing from the self-deception which we find on its face to be so paradoxical. This case presents no paradox, not even on its face. It is through *failure* to see the outcome, not design, that the swindler succumbs, whereas in self-deception of the paradoxical kind, it is of the essence that the self-deceiver purposefully brings it about that he is deceived. The swindler fails to achieve his aim; the self-deceiver succeeds. The swindler's failure does not involve loss of moral integrity; the self-deceiver's success does.

We may close this chapter by remarking some curious admissions at the end of several of the papers we have been considering. Siegler admits at the end of his paper that 'there may be other cases (than any of those he has mentioned) of reflexive deception expressions which reveal a more striking logical parallel to interpersonal deception expressions (p. 475). Canfield and Gustafson end their discussion by acknowledging (p. 35) that 'we do find cases where, in some sense, the person "knows" what he believes and asserts to be false', where what is odd in such cases is that it would take drugs, or drink, or hypnotism, or psychoanalysis to get the person to admit what he knows—'*even to get him to admit it to himself*' (my italics). A closely related suggestion of Gustafson's—made earlier by him writing jointly with McNally—is that in self-deception one of the two opposed beliefs is conscious and the other unconscious.

Such admissions inevitably raise once again fundamental questions which these papers were designed to answer. How are we to understand reflexive deception expressions which *do* show a striking logical parallel to interpersonal deception expressions? What is this odd kind of knowing such that drugs or psychoanalysis are needed before it can be expressed? How are we to understand the Freudian language of repression and the unconscious? The papers cited fail to give a satisfactory answer to these questions and curiously enough end by admitting it. It is to the task of answering these questions that we shall now proceed. I might merely add that in the course of that clarification, we shall not only account for the tendency to characterize self-deception in terms of belief and knowledge, but we shall also account for forms of self-deception undiscussed by these writers, that is, self-deception regarding such matters as one's own attitudes and wishes, and one's hopes and fears, as well as one's beliefs.

CHAPTER THREE

TO SAY OR NOT TO SAY

PARADOXES arise in connection with self-deception when we characterize it primarily in terms of belief and knowledge, or in terms of 'perception' language such as 'appear' and 'see'. It is via the 'perception' terms that a bridge is established between belief and knowledge on the one hand, and such notions as 'consciousness' and 'awareness' on the other. We might initially and loosely call this entire collection the 'cognition-perception' family—not meaning to establish a definitive classification but simply a broad suggestive one for contrast with another such 'family', the 'volition-action' family. Self-deception is readily and commonly described by use of varied combinations of terms from the 'cognition-perception' family.

For example, it is quite natural to speak of the self-deceiver as one who doesn't *perceive* his own fakery, who can't *see through* the smokescreen he himself puts up. We also say that in a way he sincerely *believes* the story he tells while 'deep inside him' he *knows* it is not true. He makes it *appear* to himself that something is so. We say the self-deceiver is *unaware* of his own deception; and, in straight psychoanalytic language, we speak of his *unconscious* wishes and fantasies. Though

34

in general this is a bag of quite various words, their remarkable interchangeability in the context of self-deception justifies, in this context, our grouping them initially as a single family of terms.

I do not propose that we eliminate the 'cognition-perception' family of terms from the analysis of self-deception. I do, however, propose a fundamental change of emphasis. This shift of emphasis I shall develop in two main stages. The first stage will consist in divorcing certain of the 'cognition-perception' terms from that family and showing, by reinterpretation, that they would be better treated for our purposes as members of the 'volition-action' family. The terms to be thus split off are 'conscious' and the variants built on this root. This first stage will in turn transform the large context in which we view self-deception, and the second main stage of my analysis will consist in a fundamentally new, 'volition-action' account of self-deception. The argument in both stages consists not in some single demonstrative proof but in the constructive elaboration of my own point of view against the background of the failure of the approaches reviewed in the preceding chapter and of the critical discussions in the later chapters of this book.

Such terms as 'know', 'be aware of', and 'be conscious of' are readily linked by the metaphor of *seeing*—the essentially passive registration and reflection to the 'mind' of what the world presents to our eyes. There is probably little need to stress the close connection, historically, between such pairs as 'know-see', 'belief-appearance'. In recent times, philosophers have become suspicious of this passive, visual imagery in connection with 'know' and 'believe'. But no such suspicion has been cast upon the language and imagery of vision in connection with 'consciousness'.

There is, of course, an element of the 'active' in vision—we turn our head and our eyes towards a scene. And we do capture some of this in the active verb 'look', and in the use of 'attention', which is of course closely related to 'conscious'. We 'turn our attention towards', and we 'turn our eyes towards'. Yet for most of the very closely related, often interchangeable terms in the group—'conscious', 'aware', 'attention', 'realize', and 'notice'—the everyday idiom stresses the passive. We 'become conscious', 'become aware', 'lose consciousness of', 'become aware of'. Realizing and noticing are expressed grammatically as transitive, but the idiom and imagery associated with them establish them as passive, as types of 'reception-concepts', as White calls them (p. 25). Finally we should note that consciousness is usually thought of as a kind of seeing rather than looking; that is, we choose the passive 'see' rather than the active 'look'.

That we become conscious we take for granted as a fundamental given; but *how* this happens is a mystery to us, a mystery so philosophically frustrating as to have been at the centre of much of Western philosophy. The solutions proposed have been various. Yet none, so far as I know, has systematically challenged the model, the language and imagery, in terms of which we characterize what it is to be or to become conscious of something. I believe such a shift is possible and for some purposes desirable. Just as we can characterize the 'feeling' of depression in terms of the imagery of heavy weight, or dark shadows, or degradedness and guilt, and yet be portraying the 'feel' of the very same feeling, so too we can portray our consciousness, *as* consciousness, in more than one way. And just as the portrayal of depression in terms of the language and imagery of guilt is far more fertile, when we reflect analytically upon the matter, than is the imagery of weight, so too, I believe, the model of consciousness which I propose will prove more fertile for philosophical analysis than is vision as a model of consciousness.

It is easy to see that vision should become the model for characterizing our being conscious of something. We are highly mobile creatures, and vision is our richest source of information for purposes of movement. Moreover, what we are conscious of—in our dealings with human beings and their artefacts—we are conscious of in good part through what we literally see. When we are conscious of talking with a person, for example, an important and typical element in this is seeing him, observing his movements in relation to his surroundings and to us. Yet it is clear that not all consciousness requires a form of vision. We are conscious of sounds and smells. We may concentrate so intently on our thoughts that, even with eyes wide open, we are not conscious of *seeing* anything. It is plain that useful as visual imagery may be for some purposes in talking of consciousness, such imagery is not necessary in all talk of consciousness.

Not only do I wish to propose a shift from visual imagery, but I also wish to shift from 'passive' imagery and language. White, in his remarks on 'becoming aware of' and 'becoming conscious of' makes a series of assertions which, taken individually and jointly, constitutes precisely the sort of account of 'conscious' which I wish to challenge. It will shortly become evident that my own theses are not strictly the contraries of what White affirms, especially since I am concerned very specifically with what I call 'explicit consciousness'. Yet one could hardly get a better sense of the direction I propose than by initially contrasting his view and mine. White says that becoming aware of and becoming conscious of

. . . are not something we do. Despite what philosophers sometimes say, there is no such thing as an 'act' of awareness or consciousness. . . . We cannot resolve or refuse to do them, nor can we do them well or badly, systematically or haphazardly. . . . It makes no sense to ask someone why he became aware of or conscious of something. . . . (p. 39).

We cannot be trained in or skilled at ('becoming aware of' or 'becoming conscious of'). (p. 40).

I propose that we turn now to a different model of explicit consciousness, that is, that we turn to a different but reasonably coherent set of imagery, metaphor, and idiom, in terms of which we shall portray what it is for us to be explicitly conscious of something. The sense of 'explicitly conscious' will become evident in the following discussion. The model I propose is one in which we are doers, active rather than passive. To be specific, the model I suggest is that of a skill. (Using such a model, it would follow, of course, that one *can* do some 'such thing' as resolve to become explicitly conscious of something, or refuse to become so, or become so effectively or ineffectively, systematically or haphazardly, for good reasons or bad; and it follows that one becomes explicitly conscious by virtue of learning, even training.)

To become explicitly conscious of something is to be exercising a certain skill. Skills, of course, are learned but need not be routinized. We are born with certain general capacities which we shape, by learning, into specific skills, some of them being quite sensitive and artful. The specific skill I particularly have in mind as a model for becoming explicitly conscious of something is the skill of saying what we are doing or experiencing. I propose, then, that we do not characterize consciousness as a kind of mental mirror, but as the exercise of the (learned) skill of 'spelling-out' some feature of the world as we are engaged in it. Like its model—language skill proper—this skill is ubiquitous among men, though in both cases the subtlety, the range, and the aptness of exercise of the skill varies markedly among individuals.

I have purposefully chosen as the name of this skill a phrase, 'spelling-out', which could not in the context be taken literally but must be taken in something like its colloquial use. For I want a phrase which provides a vivid and apt idiom, but which does not too early or too literally commit us to any particular physiological or behavioural account of the conditions of exercise of the skill in question. I do not have any such account to give.

Colloquially, to spell something out is to make it explicit, to say it in a clearly and fully elaborated way, to make it perfectly apparent. Typical uses which I have in mind are: 'He is so stupid you have to spell everything out for him'; 'He let me know without actually spelling it out'; and 'you know perfectly well what I mean—do I have to spell it out for you?'

Applied to 'becoming conscious of something', the phrase 'spelling-out' may refer, but need not, to the actual and elaborate saying out loud, or writing down, of that which one is becoming conscious of. However, the phrase 'spell-out' is intended to suggest strongly an activity which has a close relation and analogy to linguistic activity. Sometimes—but by no means always—the 'model' activity (literally making something explicit in language) is also an instance of the skill (becoming conscious) for which it serves as model. However it is clear that one often becomes explicitly conscious of something, or, to use the phrase which I now propose to use synonomously, one often spells-out something, without any evident utterance, even to oneself, or with only allusive or cryptic ones.

What the exact connection is between spelling-out and perfectly straightforward examples of linguistic activity, I do not know. I think there is always a close relation. The point of my speaking of a 'model' here is that I wish to avoid even attempting a definitive account. I am frankly delineating large areas whose boundaries are ill-defined. This is in keeping with the nature of the main enterprise, which, as I said earlier, is to sketch a very different *type* of map rather than to refine the old one.

My first thesis concerning spelling-out is fundamental to 'the new look' at consciousness which I propose. The thesis is that, generally speaking, the particular features of an individual's engagement in the world need not be, and usually are not spelled-out by him.

In stating this first thesis, I speak of an 'individual's engagement in the world'. Since I shall use this phrase frequently, as a convenience rather than as a precise technical term, I had better say a few words about the phrase now. I use it in order to characterize, in most general terms, what someone does or what he undergoes as a human subject; it is how an individual finds and/or takes the world, including himself. It is a matter of the activities he engages in, the projects he takes on, the way the world presents itself to him to be seen, heard, felt, enjoyed, feared, or otherwise 'experienced' by him. It is logically necessary that it should be typical of our description of an individual's engagement in the world that the description be cast in terms of such categories as aims, reasons, motives, attitudes and feelings, of understanding and 'perception' of the world and himself. What a person does not somehow take account of is not part of his engagement in the world, though it may have effects on the course of his engagements. Rather than stringing together uncompleted sequences like 'an individual's conduct, aims, hopes, fears, perceptions, memories, etc., etc.', I propose 'his engagement in the world' as shorthand. One might have said, '*his world*'.

The immediately crucial point is that we are not in general explicitly conscious of our engagements in the world. Or, to put the matter more positively, for an individual to become explicitly conscious of something is for him to spell-out some engagement of his; he does this either by spelling it out in general terms ('I am racing in a sailing contest'), or by spelling out some revelatory feature of the engagement ('I'm losing, my competitor's boat is about to pass me'). However it is not necessary to be spelling-out an engagement in order to be so engaged. It must be already evident that, among the various ways in which 'conscious' is used, I have selected one in which it is a very close cousin to 'explicitly aware', 'attending explicitly to'. Further comment on this point will be necessary shortly.

With exceptions (such as the performatives), there is always some special reason, over and above the simple fact of being engaged in some specific way, for taking the additional step of spelling-out this engagement. To refer to our model: We are not always saying all that we are doing; we could not. Therefore we are selective in what we say, but not arbitrarily so. The same holds true, *mutatis mutandis*, for spelling-out. When I ride a bicycle, drive a car, form and utter sentences in English, dress myself, play the violin, sit down in a chair, walk, handle my body, I usually exercise these skills well, at times with art; yet most of the time I do not spell-out, not even to myself, what I am doing. Of course normally I can, and upon occasion I will, spell-out my engagement to myself or to others, for example, that I am playing the violin, or, more specifically, that I am lowering the first finger of my left hand to the E string. When I do spell this out, it may aid or it may hinder the performance, but in any case there will be some special reason for spelling it out, e.g., I have heard myself playing a wrong note, or my finger is sore.

The point I wish to emphasize is not novel in substance, but we do not think of it, or not enough, and so we fail to appreciate its import. Rather than taking explicit consciousness for granted, we must come to take its absence for granted; we must see explicit consciousness as the further exercise of a specific skill for special reason.

Once we appreciate that we must have special reason for spelling-out, we realize that the skill of spelling-out must be larger in scope than the mere capacity to perform spelling-out. Exercise of the skill requires sizing up the situation in order to assess whether there is adequate reason for spelling-out the engagement. And the corollary of this is that in exercising the skill we are also assessing the situation to see whether there is reason *not* to spell-out the engagement. Where it happens that there are both reasons for spelling-out and reasons for not spelling-out the very same thing, these are presumably weighed against one another by the individual. Whether or not he spells-out the matter in question, or exactly how he does so if he does spell it out, will depend not only on his assessment but also upon his ingenuity in adapting to the conflicting considerations. All this is no more than we allow to be the case with complex skills generally. Skill in driving a car is not merely the ability to perform certain movements; it is also the ability to assess the possibly conflicting considerations in a situation in order to settle which movements to perform, when to do so, and precisely how. Skill in speech calls for assessing just when to speak, when not to speak, how to speak, what to say. Skill in spelling-out requires analogous assessments.

We must now remark that the exercise on a particular occasion of our spelling-out skill is itself a way of being engaged in the world; it is something we do. Therefore our first general principle applies to it: spelling-out is an activity which is not itself spelled-out except when there is special reason to do so. Generally we do not have good reason to spell-out the exercise of the skill of spelling-out. However there may on occasion be good reason. I might, for example, spell-out my finger placement while playing the violin and also spell-out *that* I am spelling-out finger placement. The occasion might be one in which I am so distractingly conscious of my finger placement as to lead me to become explicitly conscious *that* I am distractingly conscious of it.

Now let us imagine the contrasting case—and here we come to the case of most direct interest for self-deception. This is the situation in which there is overriding reason *not* to spell-out some engagement, where we skilfully take account of this and systematically avoid spelling-out the engagement, and where, in turn, we refrain from spelling-out this exercise of our skill in spelling-out. In other words, we avoid becoming explicitly conscious of our engagement, and we avoid becoming explicitly conscious that we are avoiding it. It is this case which will take us our first major step

into the region of self-deception, of the Freudian unconscious, of Sartrian Bad Faith, and of other variants
on our main theme.

At this point we may profit from pausing, slightly
retracing our steps, and filling in a bit more of the detail of what we have so broadly and quickly sketched.
I would like first to expand a bit upon the theme of
consciousness as a skill. We would do well to recall
the child's inability to focus his consciousness, to spell-
out what is relevant and needed. Children tend to be
too readily distracted or too single-minded in the focus
of their attention. They have not yet learned the skill
of turning their attention to the right things at the
right times. On the other hand, an adult's feeling for
singling out what is relevant and needs to be spelled-
out may be exceptionally sure and subtle; this is an important part of what we mean when we call him 'wise'.
For most of us most of the time, however, our skill in
making ourselves conscious of one or another feature
of our existence is like our skill in walking or talking;
these are skills we all learned moderately well at an
early age. We have by now largely forgotten our
struggles, forgotten that we had to learn these skills.
We have taken them for granted, except on those occasions when perhaps we said to ourselves, 'I must learn
to walk straighter', 'I really should practise speaking
more distinctly'; 'I must learn to concentrate.'

Although the adult can explicitly and systematically
continue to cultivate his skill in spelling-out, this has
not been a traditional concern in the Western world,
except among practitioners of religious meditational
disciplines. In Asia and Asia Minor, however, the complex doctrines of consciousness associated with meditational practice embody millenia of experience in the
cultivation of this skill. In the contemporary Western

word, psychoanalytic 'free association' may be thought of as a special spelling-out technique. More indirectly, we also develop certain aspects of our skill in spelling-out when we cultivate, for example, 'esthetic appreciation', or 'better study habits'.

Though considerations such as the preceding support the view that there is an important element of skill associated with consciousness, not all skills associated with consciousness are those of spelling-out, for not all consciousness is explicit consciousness. A few further comments are now in order concerning the meaning of 'explicit consciousness' as contrasted with the many other things to which we may refer when we use the word 'conscious' or its grammatical variants ('consciousness', 'unconscious', etc.). The word is noted for its variety of uses. To spell-out, I have said, is to be explicitly aware of; it is to pay conscious attention to. We might speak of this as the 'strongest' sense of 'conscious'. By contrast, there is the 'weaker' sense of 'conscious' in: 'Though struck a heavy blow, he remained fully conscious'; or 'he lost consciousness'. Also contrasting with spelling-out is another 'weaker' sense of 'conscious' in: 'Are you conscious that you are shuffling the cards?' 'Yes, of course, I'm perfectly conscious that I'm doing it, but that hasn't distracted me from what you are saying; I'm paying attention only to what you say and nothing else enters my mind.'

The conditions which are necessary or sufficient for the use of 'conscious' in these and other 'weaker' senses form complex, not well defined, and obscurely understood sets. Our present concern, however, is simply to isolate the chief characteristic which marks out what I have called the 'strong' sense from any of the 'weaker' ones. My proposal is that we can profitably distinguish the 'strong' from all other uses of 'conscious' by seeing the former essentially as the exercise of our skill in making explicit, in linguistic or closely related form, that which we are said to become conscious of in this 'strong' sense. A distinctive characteristic of consciousness in some of the 'weaker' senses of the word is that though we are not doing so we are readily *able* to spell-out features of our engagement when appropriate. To become conscious in the 'strong' sense of 'conscious', however, is to be actually engaged in spelling-out that which one is conscious of.

It is important to note that the model of spelling-out is the explicit expression of an engagement in language; not any use at all of language will do. We may be understanding another person's speech, but we are not necessarily spelling-out while understanding him. Nor are we necessarily spelling-out as we ourselves act purposively and skilfully in response to what he has said. Yet in both cases, though we ourselves do not speak, we are using language. A person involved in a philosophical discussion, for example, may respond to a remark having *ad hominem* overtones by resorting to ingenious, covert debating tactics designed to re-establish his self-esteem; yet he may not be explicitly conscious that he had understood this feature of his opponent's attack and is responding to it. Moreover it is generally admitted that regardless of whether there is speech, writing, or other overt use of language at a particular moment, the forms of human existence have their source so profoundly in language that a practical understanding of language—even though it be tacit—is of the essence whenever we are engaged as human beings.

Furthermore, not every instance of overt language use which appears on its face to be an instance of

spelling-out is really such. For example, an actor playing a role is not spelling-out (at least not publicly)
though he may be acting as one who is publicly
spelling-out. We do have ways which are generally but
not always reliable for judging when a person is pretending to spell-out and when he is actually doing so.
We are most likely to be deceived when the person is
self-deceived or is an exceptionally good actor and intends to deceive us. Even then, there are often ways
of detecting the genuine article. We shall discuss some
of these later.

To say that spelling-out is expression of one's engagement is to say that spelling-out is an activity which
only the agent can do for himself. The observer can
describe another person's engagement, but in doing so
the observer is explicitly telling us the way he apprehends the other person's engagement. That is, the
observer is in effect spelling-out his own engagement
in the world, the world as *he* sees it. (The actor giving
the same 'description' as lines to be delivered in his
assigned role is not spelling-out at all.)

In general, the person in self-deception is a person
of whom it is a patent characteristic that even when
normally appropriate he *persistently* avoids spelling-out
some feature of his engagement in the world. Sometimes we see this as an 'inability' to spell-out: The
self-deceiver is 'unable' to admit the truth to himself
(even though he knows in his heart it's so). There is a
kind of genuineness to his 'ignoring'; it is not simple
hypocrisy, or lying, or duping of others. Yet we also
feel that in some sense, he *could* admit the truth if only
he *would*. I believe we can now throw some light on
this paradoxical 'wilful ignorance', as Murphy, following Kierkegaard, calls it.

This inability to spell-out is not a lack of skill or

strength; it is the adherence to a policy (tacitly) adopted. 'He cannot admit it, cannot let himself become conscious of it,' here means 'He *will* not'; but the 'will not' refers to a general policy commitment and not an *ad hoc* decision not to spell it out. There is a parallel to: 'It's not that I *won't* come with you, but that I *can't* because I promised Smith I'd go with him.' The can't of self-deception is markedly different in one respect from the 'can't' of the man who promised. The promiser can't say yes, but he *can* say that he is committed not to say yes. The self-deceiver, however, is committed to say nothing on either score. Hence (1) he says nothing (does not spell-out the truth); (2) he gives us the impression that, 'in some sense', he could if he would; but (3) he also gives us the impression that he has somehow rendered himself incapable of doing it.

Why is it that the self-deceiver commits himself to avoid spelling-out his commitment, i.e., his assessment of the situation and his consequent 'policy' not to spell-out the truth? It is not merely because we do not in general spell-out the exercise of a skill. More important, the original reasons for refusing to spell-out the truth will also serve as reasons against spelling-out the prior assessment and commitment not to spell-out the truth. For to spell-out the assessment and the policy adopted would, of course, require spelling-out the engagement at issue, the very engagement the self-deceiver has committed himself *not* to spell-out. By the hypothesis, he has decisive reasons for his commitment not to spell this engagement out. Thus the reasons against spelling-out the exercise of the skill in this case will in general be the same reasons, and just as strong reasons, as those against spelling-out the engagement.

For example: I find there is strong and preponder-

ant reason for not spelling-out—even to myself—that
I have been a failure in realizing a certain ambition.
Consequently I adopt the policy of not spelling this out.
What is more, this policy obligates me as well not to
spell-out my having made such an assessment of the
situation and my having adopted this tactic. For,
obviously, to spell-out my assessment would be to spell-
out that I consider myself a failure, and that there are
reasons for not admitting this even to myself, and that
these reasons are. . . . And to spell-out the policy
adopted as a result of the assessment would also be to
spell-out the fact that, though I have been a failure,
my policy now is not to spell this out even to myself.
In either case—whether I spell-out the assessment
or the policy—it would amount to a clear abandonment of the would-be policy.

Thus the adoption of the *policy* of not spelling-out
an engagement is a 'self-covering' policy. To adopt it
is, perforce, never to make it explicit, to 'hide' it. It
is in this way notably different from not spelling something out on a particular occasion merely for lack of
adequate reason to do so. This is common, of course.
Since there is no enduring commitment not to spell-
out the matter in question, we are ready to do so on any
occasion if given reason to do so. We are also able to
spell-out *that* we have spelled it out, i.e., to become
conscious of our consciousness of something.

In general, a predictable initial result of such an
automatically 'self-covering' policy will be that in
the course of the normal occasional spelling-out of
one's engagements in the world, there will be 'breaks' or
gaps as one comes near the 'hidden' area in question:
certain memories, perceptions, desires, actions—any
of which would in general be readily spelled-out on
occasion—now are not spelled-out, even when the

occasion would otherwise be appropriate. And what adds to the potentiality of this situation for being puzzling and bothersome is that, as required by this policy, the reasons for the policy and the very fact that one has such a policy are also not spelled-out.

A self-covering policy of this kind tends to generate a more or less elaborate 'cover-story'. For a natural consequence is the protective attempt on the part of the person to use elements of the skill he has developed in spelling-out as inventively as possible in order to fill in plausibly the gaps created by his self-covering policy. He will try to do this in a way which renders the 'story' as internally consistent and natural as possible, and as closely conforming as possible to the evident facts. Out of this protective tactic emerge the masks, disguises, rationalizations and superficialities of self-deception in all its forms. If the discrepancy increases, and in any case whenever new inconsistencies between actual engagements and cover-story arise, the individual is moved to ever continuing effort and ingenuity to elaborate his story and to protect its plausibility. He may easily have the air of one who is trying to persuade himself and others. There is reason, of course, for doing all this, but he will not make it explicit to others or to himself.

The discrepancy between the way the self-deceiver has engaged himself in the world, and the declarations he makes to himself and others concerning his engagements, leads us to the question of sincerity. It is evident that an important element in the paradox of self-deception is the impression of sincerity that the observer gets when he attends to the self-deceiver's public declarations. Were the mother merely to *say* that she believes her son to be a fine boy in spite of the massive case for his being a scoundrel, we would discount this as an understandable though perhaps futile attempt to deceive us. We are more puzzled, however, when we get the impression, and finally are convinced, that she is both sincere in what she says *and at the same time* insincere.

Though the distinction between merely saying and sincerely saying is frequently invoked in philosophical discussions of language, it is rarely discussed. The distinction between being sincere and being insincere has also played a certain role, in one form or another, in contemporary Continental philosophy; but there is little attempt in these discussions to avoid paradox. We are now in a position, however, to make some non-paradoxical comments on the nature of sincerity.

The paradox of the self-deceiver's 'insincere sincerity' is generated by an ambiguity in the notion of sincerity. The ambiguity is readily specified now that we have interpreted 'becoming explicitly conscious of' as spelling-out.

We should note at once that the ascription of sincerity does not always require that the person's comportment conform with his sincere explicit declarations about his comportment. Usage varies here, though we commonly make our point clear by ascribing sincerity and then adding qualifying comment and allusion to the context. For example, we are willing to ascribe sincerity in certain cases of patent irresponsibility. Thus: 'Mr. Jones' promises mean nothing; he's quite sincere and means them at the moment of making them, but he is too thoughtless and too free with them; he is utterly unreliable.' Or: 'Jones loudly declares his loyalty on every possible occasion; and he is sincere when he does so; but it is simply a case of being swept up by emotion. He is quite undependable.' In such cases, as in self-deception, we are prone to comment that, 'It is a shallow (or superficial) sincerity.' Nevertheless, it is sincerity.

It is true that everyday usage allows such cases of 'surface' sincerity as these to be called self-deception. And insofar as we shall have elucidated this kind of sincerity-insincerity we shall have elucidated a kind of self-deception. Yet this is not in itself an intentional deceiving of oneself but is the mistake of taking the intensity of one's feeling as a guide to expressing the durability of one's commitment. We are mainly concerned with the more complex kind of self-deception, which is intentional, purposeful. In any case, my main concern at the moment is to bring out that we do have a typical use of 'sincere' in which the ascription of sincerity is not intended to imply that what a person tells us about his engagement conforms to the actual nature of his engagement.

What we do always mean to imply when we ascribe sincerity is a conformity between what the individual tells us and what he tells himself.

The ambiguity of 'sincerity' has its source in the fact that several different, independent, criteria for ascribing sincerity are usually in fact jointly fulfilled. We therefore are not clearly aware that the criteria are several and that they may not be jointly fulfilled. We are taken aback when, on occasion, only some but not all are fulfilled. We are then of two minds whether to ascribe sincerity or not. The characteristic criteria for sincerity pertain to the conformity or non-conformity of what the person tells others, what he tells himself and how he really takes things to be; and where there are discrepancies, the reason for the discrepancy and nature of the discrepancy both become diagnostic. More formally, the criteria are:

(1) It is not the case that there is an intentional

difference in the way the individual spells his engagement out to others and the way he spells it out to himself;

(2) The way he spells the engagement out to himself reflects the engagement correctly and aptly.

(3) He has not been unintentionally wrong in the way he came to express the engagement.

If (1) does not hold, the person is not sincere. (Roughly: He doesn't intend to give us the story as he gives it to himself.) If (1) does not hold but (2) does, we have ordinary lies, deceit, trickery. (Roughly: He tells himself the truth as he sees it, but he doesn't intend to tell things to us that way.) If (1) and (2) hold, but not (3), we have the 'shallow' sincerity of the irresponsibly erratic or impetuous person. (Roughly: He means to tell both us and himself the way things are, but he is unskilful in expressing matters.) If both (1) and (3) hold, then we normally characterize the person as sincere—since it is normally the case that (2) also holds. To say that (2) normally holds is, in effect, to say that normally a person tells himself the truth about his engagement.

The odd, but not so rare, case comes when (2) does not hold but (1) and (3) do: The person spells things out to others just as he does to himself, and he is unintentionally wrong in the way he spells things out to himself. Nevertheless he does not spell them out to himself as they are. Since he gives himself the very same story he gives us, we initially characterize him as sincere. Yet the more we observe him, the more we are convinced that something is abnormal, unusual, wrong; we come to see that the story he is telling both himself and us is not unintentionally wrong but purposely wrong. We now ascribe to him a peculiar, 'deeper' insincerity. Or we may say that 'in a way he believes what he says, and yet it's not genuine; he's fooling even himself.' We are puzzled by this because we have failed to think of explicit consciousness as a form of telling something. Thus we have failed to appreciate the consequences of the banal truth that what a person tells himself is highly selective, highly purposeful, namely, that he may at times purposely tell himself what is not so. The more we do appreciate that (2) does not hold in a particular case, the more we see the person as a deceiver. The more we overlook it and concentrate our attention on the fact that (1) does hold, the more fervently we insist on his sincerity.

The picture is complicated, as noted earlier, by the consequences of our tending to take seriously what we tell ourselves. (Just why we should take seriously what we tell ourselves is an important question, whose answer is not obvious. We shall take up this question at length in the chapter which follows.) The consequences are that in such cases we try to conform our subsequent conduct and our subsequent overt comments to this purposely defective version of matters. Thus the whole picture becomes increasingly complex, and the observer—as well as the agent—often must look long and carefully before being able, if ever, to disentangle the threads of the web.

A useful device for bringing out some of the distinctions I have been making is to consider a case where there is some ambiguity regarding whether the person in question is self-deceived or is a cynical, i.e., quite fully self-conscious, hypocrite. The questions we then raise in our effort to resolve the ambiguity bring out the force of the viewpoint I have been presenting. Such a case is that of Arsinoé, in *Le Misanthrope*. (We could hardly do better than to begin with an illustration by Molière, one of the earliest self-conscious masters at depicting hypocrisy, self-deception, sham, and asininity.)

Arsinoé prudishly and incessantly preaches virtue and chastity. Yet in fact, as the flirtatious Célimène reminds some mutual acquaintances, Arsinoé is merely unsuccessful in attracting men, jealous of Célimène, and in particular is bent upon robbing Célimène of her lover, Alceste. The portrait is confirmed when Arsinoé shortly arrives on stage. Under the guise of giving advice out of friendly zeal for Célimène, she vividly recounts to the latter the details of the current scandalous talk about her, thus launching obliquely but effectively a series of scathing insults against Célimène. Arsinoé later makes the same point to Alceste, joining to her virtuous narrative an eagerness to console Alceste which confirms Célimène's diagnosis.

Is Arsinoé cynically hypocritical in speaking as she does and in carrying on as she does? Or is she blind to her own falseness?

It is clear that Arsinoé is engaged in a systematic and rather skilfully realized attempt to wound Célimène. In her lengthy speeches, as in her other actions, she perceptively takes into account what will hurt Célimène, consistently prefers it, skilfully employs tactics to achieve it, and yet throughout frames her every move in the form of virtuous advice from a zealous friend. All this hangs together too well to be judged a mere coincidence, or an inconsistency rooted in error, confusion, or misperformance on her part. We feel the force of 'She is jealous and envious of Célimène, aims to hurt her and win Alceste from her, and *knows* what she's doing.' This much is essential to our judgment that Arsinoé is either cynically hypocritical or self-deceived.

If Arsinoé were to confide in some other person and admit that everything Célimène says is true, that her own prudery and friendliness are a façade designed to deceive Célimène and the others, there would be no problem. We would consider her a cynical hypocrite.

Suppose, however, that Arsinoé confides nothing of the sort to anyone (which is in fact the case). We might then look for other signs that *she* in any case is fully aware of it, that she acknowledges it at least to herself. If we found none, if we found signs, instead, that she believes what she says, that she is sincere, we should then have a case of self-deception.

Let us for a moment try to imagine as concretely as we can how we might determine that Arsinoé acknowledges to herself that she is engaged in an attempt to wound Célimène and to steal her lover. The dramatist has conventional devices he can use: Arsinoé might be left alone on stage and might engage in a soliloquy. This is the very model of spelling-out. In general we must imagine Arsinoé communing with herself in private, ruminating and reasoning as to how best to pursue her jealous aims undetected. We must picture her as not just being filled with hate but *realizing* she is, reflecting upon it, expressing explicitly to herself her project *as* destructive, *as* hate motivated, *as* a jealous one. We can express this by saying she must not only *be* jealous but must *know* she is, not only hate Célimène but *know* she hates her. 'Know' here has the force of 'express to herself explicitly'—or, as I have been saying, 'spell-out'.

If we could not convincingly picture her in the manner described, or even more, if we were convinced somehow that such a picture was untrue, we would not characterize her a cynical hypocrite. We would instead think of her as one who 'in a way' does *not* know what she is doing but believes what she says. Yet the integrity of her complex and ingenious conduct will not allow us to think that this 'in a way' connotes *mere* ignorance or thoughtlessness. We cannot believe that her not spelling-out her jealousy and hate is merely a failure to reflect which is unmotivated or non-specific to this project, a failure which derives, perhaps, from traits such as generalized intellectual laziness or incapacity. We cannot here escape the force of 'she knows what she's doing', because of the ingenuity and evidently purposeful interrelatedness of the conduct involved; yet we cannot escape the force of 'in a way she's sincere and believes what she says'. The decisive difference in the two pictures—whether or not she spells-out her project to herself—is diagnostic for self-deception.

How would we come to be legitimately convinced of the truth of one or the other picture? There is, of course, no single or simple answer. We might note that in other situations judged appropriately similar to this one, Arsinoé has at some point openly avowed such tactics. She might at some particular point in her attacks on Célimène drop the role of prude, at least for a moment, and explicitly express her enterprise in duplicity. This might be in the moment of triumph or defeat, or in response to challenge or questioning, but it would come out not as an exclamation having novelty for her but as one which expressed aloud what apparently had already been said to herself in silence. Or a situation might develop in which it would be, from Arsinoé's standpoint, highly profitable to abandon the façade for a time; if she then did so with no signs of surprise or reaction to novelty at hearing herself acknowledging the envious project as hers, we would tend to infer that what she was saying to us she had already said to herself. If she expresses herself on such an occasion in well chosen words rather than in an evidently impromptu, even incoherent, groping fashion, we may infer she had already reflected explicitly on these matters.

We also look for signs of emotion associated with the spelling-out when it finally occurs publicly; this must be emotion over spelling-out what she does, as distinguished from the emotion expressed *in* the words, or from the emotion associated with anticipation of the consequences of having said them. If Arsinoé were a cynical hypocrite, she might yet show emotion if, for example, in her final defeat, she spelled-out her hatred. But we would judge that the emotion is the hatred expressed *in* the words, and also, perhaps, that the emotion includes fear and rage over the anticipated consequences of her uncontrollable outburst. But if she were a self-deceiver, the matter would be otherwise. Her words might express rage, and might show anxiety for the consequences. But the specific evidence we would look for, if ever she did spell-out her jealousy in our presence, would be that an important part of the emotion appears to be over the *fact* that she is expressing these feelings as hers, i.e., it would be shock that *this* should be the proper characterization of her feelings and her aims.

In the case of Arsinoé, as actually presented by Molière, we do not know for sure whether she is a cynical hypocrite or a self-deceiver, and we can now say with some precision why this is so. Molière denies us the crucial test situations: she never in any way spells-out her jealous feelings and competitive aims with regard to Célimène or anyone else; hence we can never see how she would do this. Yet we cannot be sure she has not spelled-out her feelings and her aims; the actress can influence us here by indirect suggestion which leads us to guess one way or the other.

In O'Neill's *The Iceman Cometh* we find a number of instances where such crucial test situations are presented, and we then feel at once that we can make a definitive judgment. The climactic scene in the play, for example, presents the protagonist, Hickey, relating to his drinking companions his self-justifying account of how he killed his wife. He has been a travelling salesman away from home for long stretches, an unreliable husband, a heavy drinker, a gambler; he has caused his faithful wife many years of misery. Her constant pleas are met by his frequent but totally unreliable promises to change his mode of life. He concludes (I omit several interspersed stage-directions and comments by his on-stage audience):

That last night I'd driven myself crazy trying to figure some way out for her. I went in the bedroom. I was going to tell her it was the end. But I couldn't do that to her. She was sound asleep. I thought, God, if she'd only never wake up, she'd never know! And then it came to me—the only possible way out, for her sake. I remembered I'd given her a gun for protection while I was away and it was in the bureau drawer. She'd never feel any pain, never wake up from her dream. So I—

So I killed her. (There is a moment of dead silence.)

And then I saw I'd always known that was the only possible way to give her peace and free her from the misery of loving me. I saw it meant peace for me, too, knowing she was at peace. I felt as though a ton of guilt was lifted off my mind. I remember I stood by the bed and suddenly I had to laugh. I couldn't help it, and I knew Evelyn would forgive me. I remember I heard myself speaking to her, as if it was something I'd always wanted to say: 'Well, you know what you can do with your pipe dream now, you damned bitch.' (He stops with a horrified start,

as if shocked out of a nightmare, as if he couldn't believe he heard what he had just said. He stammers) No! I never—!
(pp. 240-2)

Hickey's surprise and shock at his having expressed himself in this way reveals sharply that he was in self-deception. His performance is in perfect contrast to the completely elegant and self-conscious statement made by Jean-Baptiste Clemence at the end of Camus' *The Fall*. Throughout the book, Jean-Baptiste has been engaged in confessing the sin of total egoism which *used* to be his even while, thoroughly self-deceived, he had thought himself a model of the virtues. In this book-length monologue, he confesses his old egoism and self-deception brilliantly, with style, wit, insight, a sense of the dramatic, and—apparently unwittingly— with numerous *aperçus* which illuminate the reader's inner life. His audience cannot but stand silent, fascinated, admiring and delightfully repelled, dominated by this *tour de force*—and guiltily exposed by it. As this effect grows, one suspects it is proof that Jean-Baptiste is still self-deceived, that the brilliant effect is intended to satisfy an unconfessed egoism which remains as great as ever. But at the end of the book, Jean-Baptiste explains his mysterious new 'profession', to which he has alluded a number of times. It turns out he knew quite well what he was doing.

So I have been practising my useful profession at *Mexico City* for some time. It consists to begin with, as you know from experience, in indulging in public confession as often as possible. I accuse myself up and down. It's not hard, for I now have acquired a memory. But let me point out that I don't accuse myself crudely, beating my breast. No, I navigate skilfully, multiplying distinctions and digression, too—in short I adapt my words to my listener and lead him to go me one better. I mingle what concerns me and what concerns others. I choose the features we have in common, the experiences we have endured together, the failings we share—good form, in other words, the man of the hour as he is rife in men and in others. With all that I construct a portrait which is the image of all and of no one. A mask, in short, rather like those carnival masks which are both lifelike and stylized, so that they make people say: 'Why, surely I've met him!' When the portrait is finished, as it is this evening, I show it with great sorrow: 'This, alas, is what I am!' The prosecutor's charge is finished. But at the same time the portrait I hold out to my contemporaries becomes a mirror.   (pp. 139-40)

The elegance and sophistication of this statement can leave no doubt in one's mind that this is not the first time he has spelled-out his project. He is an ex-self-deceiver who at last acknowledged his egoistic aims—and whose self-reproaches, far from leading to self-reformation, become by a brilliant *volte face* the supreme medium of expression for his now fully conscious egoism. (Of course deeper ambiguities, which it is not our concern to examine here, lie in the fact that Camus' Jean-Baptiste intended all along to confess his deception, this being the final stroke in bringing his audience to confess as well.)

Let us now review in summary but systematic form the upshot of the various discussions in this and in the preceding chapter. A brief review will help re-establish the large perspective, and it will serve to raise certain fundamental questions which are the focus of interest in the following chapter.

We reject for purposes of analysis the emphasis on belief and knowledge in such formulations as: the self-deceiver both believes and disbelieves, or, he believes one thing but knows otherwise, or, he believes when he ought to know better, or, he fulfills some (unspecified) criteria of belief even though he fully appreciates the decisively contrary evidence. Instead, we begin by focussing our attention on the notion of consciousness, and in particular that of being explicitly conscious of something; we then interpret this consciousness as the exercise of the skill of expressing our engagement explicitly in language(-like) form. We then state that the self-deceiver is one whose life-situation is such that, on the basis of his tacit assessment of his situation, he finds there is overriding reason for adopting a policy of not spelling-out some engagement of his in the world. As with any reasonably well developed skill, so in this case, too, the action suits the tacit assessment: he does not, thereafter, spell-out the matter in question; and, by virtue of this policy, he is further obliged not to spell-out the assessment or the policy. The consequence of this is that he may be observed as one who is in fact engaged in the world in a certain way, such as carrying out a destructive campaign against some person, or keeping an eye out for damaging evidence against a loved one's reputation and hiding that evidence whenever possible; yet he is unable (by virtue of his tacit commitment) to spell this fact out to himself or to anyone else. Thus when the issue is raised, he does not, cannot, express the matter explicitly at all. He is in this respect in no better position than anyone else. He tells us nothing but what he tells himself.

He does not stop at refusing to spell-out what is so. He is forced to fabricate stories in order to keep his explicit account of things and the way things really are in some kind of harmony such as will make his account of things plausible. However, he does not spell-out that he is doing this. That is, it continues to be the case that the fabrications he tells us he also tells himself.

It is because he tells us what he tells himself, a distinctive mark of sincerity, that we do say, 'He is sincere; he believes his denials.' At the same time, we observe that in other respects he shows convincing signs of being engaged in the way we ascribe to him but which he sincerely denies. The purposefulness and the often remarkable ingenuity with which he carries through his engagement lead us to insist that 'He must know what he's doing; he *must* know the truth.' The conflict in these judgments of ours ('He's sincere in his denial'—and—'He knows the truth, which is contrary to his denials') forces us to qualify each judgment and thus arrive at a characteristic (but not complete) formula of self-deception: 'In a way he's sincere, yet in his heart he knows the truth'; 'In a way he believes what he says, yet at bottom he really doesn't believe it.'

Rather than being captivated by this idiomatic language and, as philosophical analysts, persisting in such questions as, 'Does he *really* know?' or 'How can he do all this and *not* know?' we should ask instead, 'How is he engaged in the world,' and 'Does he express this engagement explicitly?' It is when we judge that there is purposeful discrepancy between the way the individual really is engaged in the world and the story he tells himself that we have the complex but common form of self-deception in which we are interested.

In everyday speech we use the word 'know' to capture the complex purposefulness of the actual engagement: 'Really', 'at bottom', 'in the last analysis', 'deep in his heart'—he *knows*. We use the weaker word, 'belief' to reflect, primarily, the very striking and normally very important feature of his performance: He is sincere in what he says, he really does tell us just what he tells himself.

Why are 'know' and 'believe' used in the everyday

idiom rather than some such language as I have used in my own analysis? Because the crux of the affair up to this point lies in the area demarcated by the phrase 'becoming explicitly conscious of', and because consciousness has traditionally been characterized in the language and imagery of knowing, believing, and perceiving. It is not that such a kinship is totally forced or illusionary. There are many contexts in which, as I have said, such language and imagery are useful. My thesis is that in the particular case of self-deception it is spelling-out, a skill aspect of consciousness, which lies at the heart of the matter. Therefore, if we wish to be able to put matters directly and non-paradoxically instead of indirectly and paradoxically, we must turn to this largely unexplored way of characterizing consciousness instead of to the familiar knowledge-belief-perception approach.

The account of self-deception which we have given up to this point is by no means complete. Indeed it raises sharply certain fundamental questions which have never been clearly formulated, much less answered, in discussions emphasizing belief, knowledge, and perception. The first and central question which it raises is: Why bother? What reason could there be for not spelling-out one's engagements even when it would normally be appropriate to do so? Or, to put the same question in somewhat more traditional language, why should an individual keep himself from becoming conscious of his own engagement in the world?

It is plain that important advantages can at times be gained by telling others what we know not to be so. A person's conduct is crucially affected by what he knows, doesn't know, thinks he knows. But in the case of the self-deceiver, if he is in any case actively, purposefully, skilfully engaged in some way, what great difference could it make to him whether he spells this out to himself or does not? We have repeatedly spoken of an individual's having overriding reason *not* to spell-out some engagement and therefore skilfully avoiding doing so. Yet what's in a word? Why should it matter whether or not we spell-out something which we are doing or experiencing in any case, and why should our refusal constitute so peculiarly human, so peculiarly demoralizing an illness as self-deception?

These questions may be raised, *mutatis mutandis,* within the framework of the psychoanalytic doctrine of defence and the unconscious, as well as within the present framework and that of the belief-knowledge doctrines of self-deception. If we are carrying on (unconsciously) in some way, why should it be of such importance that we should not become conscious of it? Why is this characterized as *defence*? The idea of unconsciousness as defence against distress has plausibility by virtue of our tacit equating of consciousness with knowledge. (What you don't know won't hurt you—at least not so far as it is in the future or in the past.) But when we recall that 'unconsciously' there *is* knowledge, or in everyday language, that 'in his heart the self-deceiver does know the truth', the question lies hidden behind the fancy word-work, but it is just as live, as puzzling as ever. If one *knows*, why bother refusing to say so at least to oneself?

As I indicated in my introductory remarks, the de-emphasis of the relation of consciousness to knowledge, and the emphasis of its relation to action, would be the crucial step, but only a step, towards a fundamental re-assessment of the context and nature of self-deception. We are now prepared to attempt this more fundamental task.

CHAPTER FOUR

TO AVOW OR NOT TO AVOW

WE have formulated a model for systematically keeping oneself from being explicitly conscious of something. In doing so we have discovered that it is a mystery why one should wish to refrain from spelling-out. These considerations, plus the fact that in general we need not spell-out our engagements in the world, inevitably raise the question: Why is it, then, that in particular instances we *do* spell anything out?

The question why we do spell-out is no doubt a basic question about the nature of consciousness. It might seem to have a prior claim to be resolved, the case of self-deception being a special case better handled subsequently. Yet, it happens that the latter is a question which is answerable directly, which also has great significance, and which fortunately is simpler to answer than the question why we do spell things out. We shall therefore proceed directly to the question why we refuse to spell-out.

The policy of refusing to spell-out one's engagement is merely the most 'visible' feature of self-deception. Though highly visible, it is a concomitant of a far more fundamental manoeuvre. The self-deceiver is one who is in some way engaged in the world but who disavows the engagement, who will not acknowledge it even to himself as his. That is, self-deception turns upon the personal identity one accepts rather than the beliefs one has. It is the hallucinator who speaks, but he will not *acknowledge* the words as his; disowned by him and undetected by others, the voice nevertheless still speaks, and so it is assigned by him to some supernatural being. The paranoid is filled with destructiveness, but he disavows it; since the presence of destructiveness is evident to him, he eventually assigns 'ownership' of that destructiveness to others. With this as his unquestionable axiom, and with 'conspiracy' as his all-purpose formula, he interprets all that happens accordingly. In general, the self-deceiver is engaged in the world in some way, and yet he refuses to identify himself as one who is so engaged; he refuses to avow the engagement as his. Having disavowed the engagement, the self-deceiver is then forced into protective, defensive tactics to account for the inconsistencies in his engagement in the world as acknowledged by him.

Having afforded ourselves this bird's eye view of the matter, we need now to retrace our steps on foot.

An individual may be born of a certain family, nation, or tradition. Yet it is something else again for that individual to identify himself with that family, nation, and tradition. He may never do so. He may grow up doing so, but then, due to changes in life-circumstance, he may grow out of one or another identity. Even more dramatically, he may as a culminating and decisive act seize a particular occasion to disavow his affiliation, his identity as an American, a Christian, or, merely, a Rotarian. As the individual grows from infancy to adulthood, he identifies himself as a person of certain traits of character, having certain virtues and vices, a certain bodily shape, having allegiances, enemies, obligations, rights, a history.

The phrase, 'he identifies himself as', certainly has some reference to discoveries the individual makes; but it refers as well to options adopted. Even with regard to something as 'concrete' and 'objective' as the body, it is interesting to note that *my* body as I identify it for myself is what the psychiatrist calls a 'body image'. He calls it my body image just because he sees that it reflects, in effect, my engagement in the world, the way I see things and take them to be, rather than the object the disinterested observer would describe.

A father announces: 'You are not my son. From henceforth I disown you.' Taken as biological description, the first sentence is false. Taken as the disavowal of identification which the second sentence reveals it to be, the first sentence can be lived up to or not— but it is not false. Although the use of 'avow' has in such cases a primary social or legal focus, it is related to the use I propose and is the model for it. The same holds true of typical proclamations such as, 'I am an American,' 'I am a union man,' 'I am no longer a Democrat.' Of the existence of such public avowals and disavowals, and of their differences from mere description, there can be no doubt. The further assumption necessary for my thesis is that something significantly analogous can be done—is commonly done— in the privacy of one's own soul. Indeed my assumption is that the analogies between what is done in self-deception (and in undeceiving oneself) and what is done in the examples just cited are so many, so interrelated, and so fundamental that we would do well to talk quite generally of self-deception in the language of avowal and disavowal, and in closely related language such as 'identify oneself as', and 'acknowledge'.

The distinction between being a certain individual and avowing one's identity as a certain person is dramatically evident in the case of the amnesiac who admits that the evidence proves he is John Jones, but who does not identify himself to himself as John Jones. Jones does not avow certain memories and commitments. As an individual he has a certain history but he does not avow that history. It is not merely that he will not avow these to us; he does not avow them to himself either. We could express all this by saying that the history in question is no longer his personal history for him. There is an important element of *authenticity* here: I refer to that respect in which, for the person before us, Jones is indeed alien, someone other. (The person before us is not sure just *who* he is, but he is sure that he does not identify himself to himself as Jones.) It is true that from the standpoint of the observer, Jones is here and is suffering amnesia. But from the standpoint of the person before us, i.e., the subject as reflected in his own consciousness, it is important to say that he is not Jones. It is this latter standpoint which I have in mind when I speak of avowal and disavowal, of identification of oneself to oneself as a certain person or as a certain person being engaged in the world in certain ways.

Depending upon the grammatical and idiomatic necessities, I shall use as interchangeable: 'Identify oneself as', 'avow', and 'acknowledge', (and as contraries: 'disavow', and occasionally 'disidentify oneself as'). I do this because the concept I have in mind is expressed by no single everyday English word or phrase. Insofar as I refer to identity as constituted by avowal, I shall speak of *personal* identity, or, simply, of the *person*. Insofar as I refer to identity without implying the avowal of that identity as such, I shall speak of the individual identity, or, simply, of the individual. To avow, then, is to define one's personal identity for oneself, not after the fact, but in that sense where we mean by 'defining one's identity' the establishing of one's personal identity in some respect. Moreover, we must include the maintaining of one's personal identity for oneself in the face of occasion for disavowal. Any such establishing or reaffirmation of one's personal identity may come to fruition in a climactic, public act; or it may be so slow and so evenly paced in its development as to seem to be natural evolution, or inherent stability in the face of stress, rather than a dramatic act. Nevertheless, avowal and disavowal are always, inherently, purposeful self-expression rather than mere happenings suffered by the person. Avowal and disavowal are accomplished by a person; they are responses by him rather than effects upon him.

The phrase 'identify oneself *with*' is normally used in connection with persons, groups, ideals. Extended uses occur: 'I identify myself with that old shack; I spent my formative years living in it, and my most intimate memories make it a symbol of my youth for me.' However I have changed the 'with' to 'as' in my phrase because I want to stress what one *is* as a result of identification and to eliminate the element of duality which remains implicit in the usual use of 'identify with'. Furthermore, what I have in mind when I use 'identify oneself as' allows reference to far more than persons, groups, and ideals; it is mainly for this reason that I also speak of avowal and 'acknowledgment'. As we ordinarily understand these terms, a person may avow or acknowledge *as his* an action, a feeling, an emotion, a perception, a belief, an attitude, a concern, an aim, a reason. In avowing them as his, as person is 'identifying himself as' one who feels, suffers, perceives, believes, etc., thus and so. The person who signs a pledge under coercion may later acknowledge the signature but may refuse to acknowledge any pledge. A person may have signed while in a hypnotic state; and later, in a post-hypnotic amnesia, he may not only refuse to acknowledge the pledge but also the signature. Were the hypnotic amnesia to be removed, he might then acknowledge the signature. Thus in speaking of avowal and acknowledgment we are concerned with an acceptance by the person which is constitutive, which is *de jure* in its force, which establishes something *as* his *for* him.

The ordinary use of 'avow' or 'acknowledge' suggests but does not require some overt expression which *is* the avowal or acknowledgment. My use, however, though it also suggests overt expression of what is avowed, does not equate the avowal with the expression of it. Avowal is an 'inner act'; which is to say that it is not in the ordinary sense an act at all, for we can never say of any piece of overt conduct that it *is* the act of avowal. Overt conduct may manifest but cannot be an avowal or disavowal, as I use these terms here. The relation is analogous to that between the conduct which manifests a decision and the decision itself.

The common notion of 'identifying oneself with' is typically used in cases where we think of the person as an already established, relatively discreet 'entity' which remains so even as it associates itself with some other, relatively discreet person, group or ideal. In more psychologically oriented discussion, however, the notion is used in a way which does not necessarily presuppose an already well formed self; instead 'identification' is the name of a development which is thought of as constitutive of a self. My use is in this respect close to the psychological use, but it is not the same. Identification, as this term is used among psychologists, is an important but special case of my 'identifying oneself as'. Indeed one of the virtues of the concept I propose is that it generalizes the psychological notion of 'identification'. It thereby allows a more fundamental approach to the understanding of personal identity, as well as to the understanding of defence and the unconscious (or their analogues in various psychological doctrines). We shall pursue these matters further in this and succeeding chapters. For the time being, however, we shall return to more direct discussion of self-deception and the role that the concept of avowal can play in an analysis of it.

Understanding self-deception as disavowal reveals, at last, the fundamental answer to our earlier question: Why is it so important not to spell-out certain aspects of our engagement in the world?

One of the marks which differentiates what is intrinsic to the identity of a person from what is not—often the principal and pragmatically sufficient mark—is that the person has the capacity for spelling-out that identity. To spell-out, as has been long noticed, is to exercise a peculiar authority, an authority intimately associated with one's existence as a particular person. The point has been both familiar and central in the Western philosophical tradition ever since Descartes. This special authority and this intimate relationship to personal identity have traditionally been attributed to the supposed 'privileged access' to the contents of one's own consciousness afforded by introspection. Essentially the same issues have been raised in more recent times by referring to the peculiar force of certain typical uses of the first person present tense of 'mental' verbs. With an authority that no one else has, *I* can speak regarding what I desire, feel, intend, experience, think, and do.

The crux of the matter is this: certain forms of spelling-out are in their implication clear affirmations by a person of his personal identity. To say in angry tones, 'I am angry with you,' or to rise and say, 'I'm leaving now,' is not only to express a certain anger or intent, it is to acknowledge it explicitly *as mine*. This is so typical, so utterly familiar, that we do not ordinarily appreciate the possibility that an individual might be angry or have a certain intent, express his anger or his intent, and yet not do so in such a way as expresses acknowledgment of them *as* his. Indeed they may be disavowed. A person may angrily say that he is not angry; and it is not uncommon to observe an individual reveal his worried state even while disavowing worry or concern. An individual may plainly be manoeuvring to leave someone's company, yet disavow any such intent. If one disavows one's loyalty to a country, one may yet continue to live there and profit from the privileges, suffer the disadvantages; but one has surrendered the right to speak *as*, e.g., an American, or to speak *for* America. Analogously, one who disavows an emotion, an intent, a deed, thereby surrenders the authority to speak as one who feels, intends, or does so and so, and he abdicates the authority to speak *for*, that is, to spell-out, the emotion, intent, or deed.

We are not yet in a position to discuss other important manifestations of avowal and disavowal. Nevertheless it may be helpful to make at least brief mention of two which will receive further attention in the following chapter and in the final chapter. One mark of disavowal is the high degree to which the disavowed engagement is isolated from the influence of everything which is avowed. The sophistication and harmoniousness of a personality has for a basis the continuous and mutual influence upon one another of the elements of the avowed. The disavowed, being relatively isolated from this system, remains proportionately static and primitive. The 'rigidity' and—in spite of a certain ingenuity in the execution—the irrationality of the disavowed engagement are the familiar manifestations of this isolation.

In addition to such isolation of the disavowed, we look for denial of responsibility. Typically, the person denies responsibility for what is disavowed; whereas to the degree that he is a responsible person, he accepts responsibility for what he avows.

Isolation, non-responsibility, and the incapacity to spell-out, with the consequences in turn attendant upon these, constitute three chief dimensions of disavowal, three profoundly significant defects of personal integrity. I do not maintain that this list of three is exhaustive. But they will furnish much grist for our mill in subsequent chapters.

I have developed the notion of avowal by ample use of what I have characterized as analogy. Yet I believe that ultimately we are not dealing here with analogies but with different manifestations of a single, generalized way of engaging in the world—what one might call, in most general terms, identity avowal. I wish only to suggest, but not even to attempt to argue, that such things as authentic avowals of loyalty to a group or nation, or authentic avowals of allegiance to ideals or causes, are manifestations of a form of response which is peculiarly human and which is, at bottom, the root of personal identity as well as social identity. However, no more shall be said here of the latter, since the primary concern of this book is directed far more to the question of personal identity.

My remarks concerning avowal and its role in self-deception clearly raise questions concerning the ambiguities in such terms as 'self', 'himself', 'the person', 'I'. Is the 'I' who disavows anger the 'same' as the 'I' who is angrily engaged in the world? To this, and to a number of other such questions readily suggested by the analysis of self-deception in terms of avowal, the answer must initially be 'yes, and no'. The objective of the following remarks in this chapter is so to re-describe the situation that we can correctly give either yes or no answers to appropriately transformed questions. In doing this we shall have again enlarged the context within which we see self-deception; in fact we shall also have arrived by the back route, as it were, at a viewpoint which reveals new aspects of personal identity and personal responsibility.

It is worth remarking that the complex of issues concerning personal identity is not raised in the series of analytical philosophical papers discussed in Chapter II. Yet I do not think that any adequate analysis of self-deception can avoid an examination of such issues. Writers like Sartre, Freud, and Kierkegaard have in effect argued that self-deception is an illness peculiar to subjectivity, to self-hood, that it is alienation of self from itself, evasion of being oneself. In the broad spectrum of contemporary Anglo-American analytical philosophy, however, I know of only one attempt at resolving the puzzle of self-deception by extensive reference to the concept of the self. This attempt is the late Arthur Murphy's, and it is to be found in his chapter on 'The Moral Self in Sickness and in Health.'

Murphy defines the problem he sets himself in this chapter as that of trying to understand how to meet certain objections to the doctrine he has been elaborating. Murphy's own doctrine of the self leads him to state with sympathy that 'once the good is known the rational man cannot but prefer it, for it is as a greater good or lesser evil that he prefers one thing to another insofar as he is rational, and it is as rational that, as a practical agent, he is himself' (p. 138). The prima facie objection is the familiar one: What of those who choose, or at least seem to choose, evil? To meet the objection, Murphy begins by relying on the notion of 'wilful ignorance', a notion he systematically develops as the originally Kierkegaardian emendation of the Socratic thesis (p. 140). Murphy refers explicitly in this context to Sartre's account of 'self-deception', and, in the course of the same discussion, he talks about Freud's views. It is plain, therefore, that in discussing wilful ignorance as the root of the 'sickness of the self', Murphy is focussing on much the same issues which we have discussed in connection with 'self-deception'. It is interesting to see that casting the problem of self-deception in terms of sickness of the self (rather than incompatible beliefs) immediately and explicitly leads to introducing the themes of Existentialist thought and of psychoanalysis—even in the writings of a Murphy, whose basic style and background are so antipathetic to these 'schools' of thought.

Murphy speaks of 'the perversity of a self that "wills" (or acts) against the practical commitment of the good it somehow knows, even in the effort to remain in ignorance of it' (pp. 144-5). This kind of irrationalism, says Murphy, cannot be ignored. Though in general he stresses the rationality of the practical agent, Murphy says he proposes to build his case upon this kind of perverse irrationality: only a self that is already a rational agent (as Murphy uses the phrase) can be irrational in this particular way. Murphy, borrowing a phrase from Kierkegaard, acknowledges that there is a kind of 'double-mindedness' about it. This self presupposes what it rejects. Only a self which was deeply committed to rationality would take the trouble to engage in rationalization. Murphy refers to the Sartrian language: the self which rationalizes also 'is what it is not'. Murphy, however, considers this as Existentialist 'double-talk' or 'jargon', and rather than 'indulge' in it, he prefers 'to direct attention to the facts it darkly describes. . . .' (p. 145).

Murphy offers as one answer to the question how a self can act against what it sees to be its good: 'the spirit is willing but the flesh is weak' (p. 146). However he adds that there are also cases where what the agent sees as his good is not willed by him, and where this is not because of lack of stamina but because the *spirit* 'is not willing'. The latter are 'harder cases' to explain, says Murphy (p. 146).

How shall we account for these 'harder cases', for 'a spiritual defiance' of what we see we should do? The problem is complicated by the fact Murphy views the will not as an 'internal agency' which makes us act, but as 'the self as practical agent in action'. Such a spiritual defiance of the good must therefore be considered as that of a 'self that is divided against itself' (p. 146). That such a condition does really occur, Murphy assures us, and he adds that it is 'not really difficult to understand' (p. 146).

But it is difficult to understand Murphy's subsequent explanation of a self divided against itself. Murphy begins by making a distinction which, he says, is the 'essential fact to see here'. In the kind of case in question, he says, it is not good that is rejected but ' "good" —that which is so-called by the lay or clerical authorities or by convention but which the individual who rejects it will not, in its claim to normative cogency, accept' (p. 146). Furthermore, this 'so-called good' is rejected in favour of some alternative which the individual is 'genuinely concerned to justify as at least *his* good and as such worth achieving' (p. 147).

By this point something seems to have gone wrong with Murphy's account. It is clear that there is nothing of our paradoxical self-divided-against-itself here. Here we have simply the person who is at odds with the 'lay or clerical authorities' or with 'convention', but he is not at odds with himself.

Having eliminated the baby along with the bathwater, Murphy now gradually re-introduces the baby (*and* the water, however). What was referred to as being 'genuinely concerned to justify' an alternative good is soon alluded to by Murphy as 'rationalization' (in quotes in Murphy's text). 'The worse', we are told, 'must be made to appear the better. . . .' (p. 147). Murphy's use of 'rationalization' and 'appear' are crucially ambiguous here: do they mean, respectively, 'to provide genuine reasons' and 'to *be*', or do they mean 'to provide pseudo-reasons' and 'to appear to be but *not* really to be'?

Murphy then proceeds immediately to say (1) that the 'evil' chosen by the person 'must be presented' as 'authentically good' for 'those who count'. And (2), he immediately offers the example of the gangster who 'by this formula' is in his own eyes an 'enterprising American' (p. 147). But here, too, we are left in the dark as to whether being 'presented as authentically good' means '*is* authentically good'. The example of the gangster suggests that the intended answer is, no. The fact that this is shortly afterwards called self-deception by Murphy supports this interpretation. Further, Murphy again refers to this as 'rationalization', and finally he says that rationalization is insincere.

The conclusion we must draw at this point is that Murphy means that the self-deceiver makes the evil *appear* (authentically) good to himself through a kind of insincerity with himself, all the while being in truth committed to something other than this as the genuine good.

We are now back at the paradoxical and genuine notion of self-deception. It is, as Murphy now says, insincerity with oneself (not merely dissent from conventional values); it is 'wilful ignorance', the 'willed exclusion of the consideration that would expose' (p. 147) the inadequacy of one's rationalizations. It is paradoxical to propose that one *wilfully* excludes whatever would expose one's rationalizations, for this presupposes that one is cognizant of those rationalizations *as* such, that one is able to identify counter-considerations, and then—precisely to the extent that one has identified the counter-considerations and acknowledged their force as such—that one refuses to consider them! This is indeed a self divided against itself.

Murphy now suggests (but does not elaborate) the thesis that we can manage this feat if: 'we can work ourselves up' into such states as anger, pride, self-pity, self-righteousness, thereby becoming 'effectively blind' to considerations which would disclose the authentic moral status of our comportment (p. 148). This proposal, cryptic as it is, gains what plausibility it may have from the ambiguous phrase 'work ourselves up'. To the extent that this means that we are overcome by these states, it amounts to imputing lack of emotional self-control, or weakness of character; and these, of course, may lead to moral blindness. This is at most the 'innocent' form of 'wishful thinking'. But when such 'blindness' persists and continuously adapts itself, even as emotion recedes, even as occasion for correction lies at hand, we must presume something more. If 'working ourselves up' means, in effect, purposely emoting at strategic moments with the intent to keep oneself 'blinded', then Murphy is asserting that the moral insight co-exists with the blindness, and that the insight and the blindness are fused in a single intention —and this remains paradoxical.

One might interpret Murphy as proposing still a different thesis: that a morally binding fever of emotion is produced with intent, but that the 'fever' is a temporally subsequent effect which, once produced, maintains itself, so to speak, and overwhelms and expunges the truer insight which had been present in the original intent. With this interpretation we are left with a person who has caused himself to be morally blind, who now *is* morally blind, but who is not now deceiving himself. This may come about in two ways. One is analogous to that of the person who knowingly and frankly gets himself drunk in order to blur his present, distressingly clear moral insight. He has not so much deceived himself at any moment as he is simply blind at a later moment due to his clear-sighted and wilful conduct at an earlier moment. The other way in which the same result may be brought about is analogous to the case of the person who maintains with a certain surface sincerity that the next small drink will surely be his last, knowing in his heart that the end will be as he secretly wants it to be—the moral release of intoxication. In this case, too, the end-state, once achieved, is not self-deception but alcoholically induced mental stupor. But in this case the final, non-self-deceptive, state is *induced* through self-deception.

Murphy's final effort to unravel the tangle consists in his asking not *how* we accomplish self-deception ('willed ignorance'), but why we 'will to be ignorant'.

Here he turns to the theme of the self as 'practical agent', this self being, he says, a creation, a synthesis of elements, an achievement of some degree of integrity of being. Viewed in this way, the self is easily seen to be subject to its peculiar sickness—the failure fully to achieve the integrity and synthesis towards which the half-formed or ill-formed self points.

We are back to the self divided against itself. But the nature of the division still eludes us. At once Murphy expands on this as 'will' ('practical doing') being 'at odds' with understanding. ' . . . (The practical agent's) "lower nature" which, as a self, he can no longer control, impels him to behaviour for which as a moral agent he feels a sense of guilt' (p. 150). It appears that, once again, we are no longer dealing with self-deception but with the very kind of irrationality which Murphy earlier dismissed as not being one of the class of 'hard' cases. We are back to the case where the spirit is willing but the flesh is weak. We are back to lack of self-control, not self-deception. That the former may be a motive for the latter is indubitable, but allusion to this motive for self-deception does not clarify the paradox within self-deception.

Throughout his windings and turnings, Murphy returns to the theme of the self as an achievement, a synthesis, and to self-deception as a failure of this synthesis. In this I believe he is fundamentally on the right track. Furthermore he sees rationality as central to the self, and I think he is correct here, too. This is not to say, however, that rationality is the sole distinctive and essential feature of the self. Murphy's error lies in the assumption that it is the rational character of the self which is central to understanding self-deception. Because of this rationalistic bias Murphy repeatedly returns in the course of his tortuous analysis to the theme of knowledge and ignorance, and to the derivative theme of the rational self as weak and the fleshly self as powerful. These themes are not adequate for elucidating the nature of the sickness he so well describes as a self divided against itself.

What Murphy fails to appreciate is the implication of his own thesis that the self is a synthesis which emerges in time, an achievement, 'built' by the individual out of materials which 'are in many ways recalcitrant to such ordering' (p. 149). The thesis that man '*makes* (italics in original) his nature as a moral being . . .' has as its too little appreciated corollary that man *rejects* materials, that he excludes material from the self as well as accepting, incorporating, and synthesizing.

We must seek now to establish more precisely what are the 'materials' which man uses, what is it for an individual to 'possess' these materials *as* material ready for incorporation into, or exclusion from, a unified self; and we must ask what is the significance of such acceptance or rejection. For it is not ignorance or temptation but the authenticity of such exclusion from a self, or inclusion within a self, which is at the core of that spiritual disorder we call self-deception.

The phenomena of self-deception (I include here, as usual, the phenomena covered by such terms as Sartre's '*mauvaise foi*', and Freud's 'defence') can be consistently interpreted within the framework of the doctrine that the self is a synthesis, an achievement by the individual, something 'made'. Avowal is the 'missing link' which is implicit in the doctrine of the self as synthesis. In order to show how this is so, I do not propose to present a tightly woven theory in a technical language, but to offer a broad and rapid sketch of the familiar course of the emergence of the self, a sketch unified by the view that the self is a synthesis, a creation. Naturally I shall highlight those features I have claimed are essential to self-deception. (The reader who desires to supplement his own observations in reflecting upon the following sketch is referred to such standard descriptive works as Gesell and Ilg's *Infant and Child in the Culture of Today*.)

Before achieving a relatively coherent unity as a self, the child learns relatively specific forms of engagement in the world. First these are quite rudimentary: using a spoon, opening a door, buttoning a coat. Then he learns complexes of interrelated motive, reason, emotion, relevant objectives, appropriate means, and, where relevant, moralistic judgmental tone. We do not normally see the latter sorts of specific engagements, at least not clearly, even at the age of two or three years. For example, the two-year-old does not rise to an insult by adopting a vengeful policy, selecting and using appropriate means to carry out his policy; nor perforce does he feel guilt for this. By the age of three years one may see intimations of this, and by the age of five such learning is usually evident. The five-year-old has learned, for example, to appreciate both time of day and his own hunger as jointly justifying seating himself at table and eating in certain generally prescribed ways, to the ends of satisfying hunger and pleasing his parents, all the while enjoying the moralistic reaction of feeling 'good' (rather than 'naughty'). He has also learned that under certain conditions an object is his property, permanent or temporary, and that seizing it without his permission by his peers is occasion for anger on his part, for retaliatory action accompanied by a moralistic reaction which includes quite typically his feeling 'naughty' or 'bad', as well as feeling 'righteously indignant'. (The rationality of these moralistic reactions is characteristically not questioned; the pattern as a whole is learned, and only later, when a unified self and its larger perspective can be brought to bear, do moral criticism and personal moral judgment emerge.)

Yet even the four- or five-year-old, capable as he may be of engaging at last in a particular complex activity for childish reasons, with childish aims and methods, and in childish moods, still does not manifest an enduring centre, a personal core whose unity colours and shapes his various particular engagements. He shifts, eccentrically, at the behest of others, or because something in the environment distracts him, or because he is fatigued, from one project to another, each being relatively unaffected by the others; any one of these engagements is not noticeably judged by him with reference to the others, nor is it markedly coloured by them. The overall unity of personal style and attitude, the inwardly governed and relatively smooth transition, are as yet absent. The psychoanalysts tell us that in ways too subtle to be readily apparent, a unified core of personality evolves, at least in nucleus, by age two and a half to four (the oedipal phase); and the careful observer can even then notice certain gross patterns of temperament or style. Yet for the layman the evolution of a noticeable autonomous governing centre does not usually begin to manifest itself until the early school years. Indeed this is a traditional sign of readiness for school beyond the nursery or kindergarten level. At this period the child is able, at least for periods of time and with rudimentary success, to carry on autonomously. One engagement leads into, blends into, another; the child is not *merely* 'negative' or else 'obedient', but shows a degree of independence in his response to external demands. There begins to emerge a large 'plot' determined from within. After a few years, even the immediate moralistic reactions ('nice', 'naughty', 'shame', 'good', 'bad') soften—though this is one of the last stages of the process—as one specific form of engagement is related to another, as a coherent self emerges, and as the generality and many sidedness of judgment which this makes possible nourish more 'personal' moral response.

These very general comments, as I have said, are intended merely to remind the reader of certain large lines of development, readily apparent to all, but rarely if ever contemplated in the context of an analysis of self-deception. Some explicit metaphor can help bring out the crucial element in this transition to autonomy, this movement in which, as I shall say, an individual becomes fully a person.

The metaphor of the self as a community rather than a collection is an ancient one and an apt one. It deserves comment here. My account, which allows use of this metaphor, diverges from the more familiar use of the metaphor in the way I identify the members of the community: In Plato as in Murphy, the members are such as Reason and Appetite, or in more Christian terms, the 'Spirit', the 'Flesh'. In the community of the self, as I see it, however, the members are the various originally independent forms of engagement, the rudimentary but unified complexes of reasons-motive-feeling-aim-means-and-moralistic reaction. When these atomic forms acquire citizenship in the community of a self, they are significantly transformed by virtue of the mutual interaction and interdependence, yet they do not entirely lose their distinctive character or quasi-autonomy. Ideally, the uncivilized and unsocialized child becomes a civilized member of the community, and yet he retains his individuality; and, analogously, the primitive and independent forms of engagement are ideally integrated with each other within a self, and they remain specific even though subtly transformed, even though serving as a medium in which the one person is constantly expressing himself.

Since we are frankly dealing here in metaphors, it cannot hurt to vary the image slightly and see this achievement of self-hood as akin to the affiliation of two independent persons with each other as husband and wife; we must imagine the forging of an ideal marriage in which individuality is not lost, and which continues to reflect not only the individuality of the partner, but, more and more, a novel unity which is the centre for both. Whether in committees, marriages, or selves, deviations from ideal are of course common.

The child learns many particular forms of engagement; he 'plays' various roles continually, zestfully, as well as being tutored in some by adults. Some forms of engagement remain merely projects realized and then forgotten, roles learned and then abandoned. However certain forms of engagement—or even some particular ones—are taken up into the ever-forming, ever-growing personal self, and they are modified as they become more and more an integral part of this 'synthesis'. To take some engagement into the personal self is not an act of physical incorporation (though Freud showed how important this image is in this connection). To take something into the self is an 'act' which our notion of personal identity presupposes. It is to commit oneself to treat something *as* a part or aspect of oneself, or as something inherent in the engagements which the person avows.

If there were no such thing as a person's *acknowledging* some identity as his and certain engagements as his, and disavowing other identities and engagements, there would be neither persons nor personal identity. Without this, man would be at most a highly co-ordinated, even highly intelligent animal, engaged in a sequence of pursuits in entire and inevitable unself-consciousness. Such creatures might be numbered or named, and even referred to as 'persons', but they would not have the capacity for the moral or spiritual life.

Generally speaking, with the emergence of the person in the individual, there is a tendency for increasing correlation between what is avowed by the person and the actual engagements of the individual. It is in terms of the tacit ideal of perfect harmony in this respect that we tend to assess the individual. We are less disturbed by the discrepancies we see in the child; children are only 'half-formed'; they will 'grow up' and 'grow out of it'; meanwhile, they go in a hundred directions, and we are patient of this. Yet even for children we do have certain age-level expectations.

It can come about, for child or adult, that our expectations are not met. And, in particular, it happens—witness the self-deceiver—that an individual will be provoked into a kind of engagement which, in part or in whole, the person cannot *avow* as *his* engagement, for to avow it would apparently lead to such intensely disruptive, distressing consequences as to be unmanageably destructive to the person. The crux of the matter here is the *unacceptability* of the engagement to the person. The individual may be powerfully inclined towards a particular engagement, yet this particular engagement may be utterly incompatible with that currently achieved synthesis of engagements which is the person.

The capacity to pursue specific engagements independently, as autonomous projects, without integration into the complex unity of a personal self, is, as we have noted, an early and a fundamental capacity of the human being. We may now add that the phenomenon we classify under such headings as 'self-deception', 'defence', and '*mauvaise foi*', are 'regressions' to this form of engagement; they manifest our capacity for such isolated engagements even after the emergence of a personal self, and in spite of unacceptability to the person. We judge from the totality of the conduct that the individual is engaged in a certain way, and he may even show signs of shame or intense guilt; yet we note what are in fact the characteristic features of disavowal: the person does not speak of the engagement as his, he does not speak *for* it, and he seems sincere; the engagement seems to exist in a certain isolation from the tempering influence of the person's usual reasonableness, his tastes, sensitivities, values; the person accepts no responsibility for being engaged in this way. On occasion we also distinguish the reparative measures being taken in order to minimize the discrepancies.

Let us imagine, for example, an individual who is intensely angered by his employer's attitude towards him. The individual, we shall suppose, is unable to rid himself of this reaction. Yet such anger towards such a person is radically unacceptable to this person. An unprincipled and humiliating subservience in spite of the anger would also be unacceptable, and in any case it would continue to bear the stigma of being his own anger, even if acknowledged to no one but himself. As a least evil, the person disavows the unquenchable anger and aggression: It is not 'I' who am angry; from henceforth I disassociate myself from it; it is utterly repugnant to me. By rejecting identity with the anger, the person avoids responsibility, but he also surrenders all authority and direct control.

Nevertheless, the fact remains that the individual is thereafter left to pursue this aggressive relationship as an isolated project. It readily manifests itself in harmful action and hurtful words towards the employer. There may be moralistic guilt reactions associated with it. These, too, are of course disavowed, though the evident manifestations of mood may be rationalized as 'depression' or undirected sulkiness.

Because of the moralistic guilt reaction, and also for purposes of protective camouflage against interference, the individual may initiate ameliorating and cover-tactics: he may find or invent some role to play—perhaps the role of the completely respectful and friendly employee. This may, by its practical effect, require a modification of the manner of being aggressive, or it may at least soften the practical impact of the effects of being aggressive. There is no problem, in general, in supposing that an individual can invent congenial explanations or play various roles; what we further assume here is that these activities, too, are disavowed. The upshot is that the 'lines' delivered may superficially appear as spelling-out, but the person is not in truth spelling-out. Since the role is disavowed, he cannot spell-out. However the individual can speak more or less skilfully the lines which he has learned would in general be appropriate for a friendly and respectful employee. Since this is a generalized role rather than a personal response, and since the self-deceiver may not be a very good actor, we notice a certain artificiality in his friendliness, a tendency to overdo and 'ham' it, a certain insensitivity to the subtleties peculiar to the situation, a stereotypy in manner.

Of course the success of such cover-tactics by the individual depends—as we know—on choosing a role which the individual can reasonably effectively play

in the circumstances and in spite of his contrary inclinations. If the conflict of inclinations is too intense,
we will see not only an erratic performance exhibiting
the signs of 'forced' friendship, but along with this
eruptions of 'unintelligible' anger. Aided by circumstances and his own intelligence, however, the individual will soon find ways of ameliorating conflict and
frustration by incorporating the angry, aggressive aims
into the role of the friendly employee. 'Helpful friendliness' then becomes 'accidentally' inopportune and hurtful; 'respect' becomes so irreproachably complete as to
annoy and embarrass the employer, exposing the
latter's defects all the more sharply by their very
contrast with the well selected excessive compliment.
The 'best of intentions' leads to the most damaging of
results. Equilibrium lies in achieving maximal aggressive satisfaction consistent with bearable guilt and
minimal threat of interference. In the latter connection
it should be noted that the threat to the self-deceiver's
personal integrity is minimized: the friendly role is
consistent with what in general he might avow as his.
And until the day of his employer's short temper, or
dawning insight, there is no retribution from the
employer.

Though the role-responses happen in a particular
instance not to be genuinely evoked in the person, the
role, as had been noted, is likely to be one which is
generally compatible with the person's integrity. Therefore it may be that the defensive use of a particular
role is congenial for a variety of 'cover' purposes, that
after a time it becomes habitual and is then remarked
as a characteristic of the individual. Provided it still
is somehow evident to the observer that this is a response 'apart', a way of acting which retains, at bottom, its relatively isolated, rigid, and not authentically

personal character, we see it as a certain sort of 'personality trait' or 'mannerism', the sort which we tend to label in today's quasi-psychological fashion, a 'neurotic' or 'defensive' mannerism or trait. Our everyday distinctions are not too clear here, but, at the extremes in the spectrum of personality traits, we distinguish the 'truly' friendly person at one pole, and, at the other pole, the person who is unyieldingly and undiscriminatingly 'friendly' to all—but really friendly to none.

In concluding this and the previous chapter, it may be well to recall that throughout the analysis of self-deception in terms of avowal and in terms of the skill of spelling-out, I have not relied on the terminology of the 'cognition-perception' family to make the essential discriminations. Rather than the paradox of knowing ignorance, I have treated as central the capacity of a person to identify himself to himself as a particular person engaged in the world in specific ways, the capacity of a person to reject such identification, and the supposition that an individual can continue to be engaged in the world in a certain way even though he does not acknowledge it as his personal engagement and therefore displays none of the evidences of such acknowledgment.

CHAPTER FIVE

SARTRE AND KIERKEGAARD

1. *Sartre and Mauvaise Foi*

SARTRE stresses the aspect of 'choice', of will, of purpose, of the 'inauthentic' rather than the unknown, in dealing generally with problems of the kind that concern us here. Moreover, he is deeply concerned with analysing the moral context of self-deception. Thus Sartre conceives the problem in a different way, and in certain respects in a far more comprehensive way than do recent analytical discussants (except for Murphy). In spite of this, Sartre agrees that 'The essential problem of *mauvaise foi* is a problem of belief' (p. 67). For Sartre, self-deception is a matter ultimately of the 'art of forming contradictory concepts. . . . *Mauvaise foi* seeks to affirm their identity while preserving their differences' (p. 56).

This specific false assumption, that *mauvaise foi* does aim at belief, leads Sartre into as much of a dead-end of paradox as it does the analytical philosophers we have discussed. Sartre's phrase, '*mauvaise foi*', reflects his basic viewpoint—that we are dealing here with a matter of bad faith rather than knowledge and ignorance; and the examples he discusses, clearly cases of self-deception, afford him opportunity to display his genuine insight into the phenomenon. Yet his specific doctrinal formulations lend plausibility to Kaufman's translation of '*mauvaise foi*' as 'self-deception' rather than the literal, and ultimately preferable, 'bad faith'.

In spite of his failure to present an adequate analysis of the structure of *mauvaise foi*, Sartre's awareness of moral context and psychological detail is so acute that we can profit from relating it to our own earlier analysis and deepening both in the process. We shall begin by examining critically the first illustration that Sartre presents in his chapter on *mauvaise foi*, the case of the disingenuous flirt (pp. 55-6).

In Sartre's illustration, a woman goes out for the first time with a particular man; she 'knows' his intentions and 'knows' she will have to make a decision, but she 'does not want to realize' the urgency of it, 'does not apprehend' his conduct as 'an approach', 'does not want to see' the 'possibilities of development' in his conduct. She 'restricts' his behaviour to what it is in the present. The man takes her hand in his. To leave the hand is to consent to flirt. To withdraw it is to break the troubled, unstable harmony which gives the hour its charm. The young woman leaves her hand there, but she does not 'notice' this. She does not notice because it happens that she is at this moment all intellect, drawing her companion into the loftiest regions of speculation. The body is divorced from the soul. The woman is in *mauvaise foi*, and she has used various procedures to maintain it.

Sartre puts the problem of *mauvaise foi* in terms reminiscent to us from our own earlier discussion: 'How can we believe by *mauvaise foi* in the concepts we forge expressly to persuade ourselves?' Sartre emphasizes in his own terms the dilemma we have already noted in other terms: 'We must note in fact that the project of *mauvaise foi* must itself be in *mauvaise foi*. . . . At the very moment when I was disposed to put myself in *mauvaise foi*, I was of necessity in *mauvaise foi* with respect to this same disposition. For me to have represented it to myself as *mauvaise foi* would have been cynicism; to believe it sincerely innocent would have been in good faith (*bonne foi*)' (pp. 67-8).

We must ask—as does Sartre—where and how does it all start? How does one initially get into *mauvaise foi*, and how is it possible that we could intentionally initiate it without knowing what we are doing, at least at the moment of the first step? Furthermore, assuming with Sartre that consciousness is 'transparent' and 'unified', that in the nature of the case there can be nothing unconscious in consciousness, how can we get into a condition where we do not know what we know?

Sartre's answer to the first question is that the original project in *mauvaise foi* is itself a 'decision in *mauvaise foi*'; however it is not a 'reflective, voluntary decision', but a 'spontaneous determination of our being'. 'One *puts* oneself in *mauvaise foi* as one goes to sleep and one is in *mauvaise foi* as one dreams' (p. 68). This answer, as it stands, reflects the truth. Sartre's analogy with going to sleep is an inspired one, for it reminds us that things of this sort do happen, that self-deception is not alone in appearing odd when viewed from the standpoint of intent, and of action and responsibility. Yet the insight it gives is still by way of relatively distant analogy and of paradox. His answer seems to tell us that on the one hand the birth of *mauvaise foi* is something that happens, that is not a clear-cut intentional doing, that on the other hand one does 'put' oneself into it, and what occurs thereafter ('dreaming') is motivated self-expression.

Equally unhelpful is Sartre's answer to the question as to how we can maintain ourselves in the condition of *mauvaise foi* once we have entered into it. Can one and the same 'unified' consciousness both believe and not believe? On this issue, Sartre's concluding definitive words are that the 'structure' of *mauvaise foi* is 'of the metastable type' (p. 68); it consist in an 'inner disintegration in the heart of being' (p. 70). In short, we are here given esoteric labels rather than a resolution of the dilemma.

I have, of necessity, simplified Sartre's position. There is a complex context of ontological doctrine into which it fits and on which I do not propose to expatiate here. I have attempted to avoid injustice to the implications of that doctrine with respect to the immediate issues. I must mention, however, certain theses of his which are directly relevant to the issue at hand and which allow us to construct in Sartre's own terminology a more informative account of *mauvaise foi*.

We can begin with the thesis, accepted by Sartre, that *mauvaise foi* is characteristically a refusal by Consciousness to accept responsibility for the world as Consciousness has engaged itself in that world. I propose to re-state elements of the flirt-situation in terms of disavowal and in the relevant Sartrian language.

The hour is entered into with flirtatious designs; but the woman disavows any such designs. As an individual and a woman she responds in the appropriate way on the appropriate occasion. Yet encouraging a sexual liaison is for this particular person radically inconsistent with her personal identity: '. . . the desire cruel and naked would humiliate and horrify her' (p. 55). Does she 'know' what she's doing and what her hand is doing? If conduct carried on skilfully and designed to realize flirtatious ends is the test of knowing, she knows. If it is a mark of knowing that she manoeuvres her hand with perfect control in such a way as to make it enticingly accessible while refraining from any explicit sexual overture, then she knows what she is doing with her hand. Sartre calls this pre-reflective consciousness, or 'nonthetic' knowledge.

If, on the other hand, the test of knowledge is the ability to 'introspect', if it is to be able to spell-out the flirtatious project as hers, if—to use Sartre's language—she is to posit it as an object of reflective consciousness and thus to have 'thetic knowledge' of it, then the woman does not know. For, having disavowed the project as hers, she has committed herself to refusing to spell-out (reflect upon) her project, and this commitment is in turn barred from being reflected upon, for reasons of the sort presented in Chapter Three. Thus she chooses to keep everything pre-reflective; or, in a different language, this exercise of the skill of spelling-out consists in keeping the entire affair unspelled-out.

Furthermore, her disavowal of the flirtatious project —and hence of the purpose of her skilful use of her hand—constitutes her as unwilling to accept responsibility for the project. Finally, since the Self, for Sartre, is a construction of reflective consciousness, the flirtatiousness is thus effectively excluded from the Self. This is the 'inner disintegration' of which Sartre speaks. The Self, as Sartre says, is indeed the product of an 'impure reflection', a reflective consciousness which is irresponsibly biassed towards a fixed conception (her Self as 'pure' and 'chaste'). Consciousness (the individual) freely engages itself in a flirtatious project. The fixed system of the Self does not allow for such a project. There is a refusal by Consciousness to reflect upon the incriminating features of conduct by virtue of this demand rooted in the Self.

If we ask how, if ever, reflection could become 'pure', how Self and freedom could become reconciled, I think we can now see the outlines of an answer in Sartrian terms. Sartre hints, in several much remarked footnotes and asides, that such an answer concerning our 'salvation' exists; but he himself gives no further clue to it in *Being and Nothingness*. The answer, from the perspective of *Being and Nothingness*, is that an authentic Self, rooted in 'pure' reflection and in good faith, will exist when, if ever, the freely chosen projects of Consciousness coincide with the enduring system which is the Self. And indeed this ideal, formulated in Sartre's terminology, turns out to be a version of an age-old spiritual idea: the perfect virtue of a person who does the right and the good not through obedience to the Law and self-discipline, but as the issue of his spontaneous response to the situation and the moment. This is not only a Christian ideal, it is also to be found in the Jewish tradition, in a variety of mystical traditions of East and West; even such a ceremonial and self-discipline oriented teacher as Confucius could be quoted by his disciples as saying: 'At seventy I could follow the dictates of my own heart; for what I desired no longer overstepped the boundaries of right.' Another way to express the same ideal is to speak of a person who accepts himself totally, an individual who freely, spontaneously, does what in fact is always an expression of his personal integrity. This would be a Consciousness which speaks with one voice, one true voice; it would be an essential and distinctive aspect of what Kierkegaard calls that 'purity of heart' which excludes 'double-mindedness'. (Kierkegaard sees, however, as the Sartre of *Being and Nothingness* does not, that this is only one aspect of the saving ideal. We shall take up the issue again in discussing Kierkegaard, and also at the end of the last chapter.)

We should note, for the sake of completeness, that the flirtatious young woman also adopts a self-defensive role: she is the 'intellectual conversationalist'. Of course she disavows this role; just as she carries on her amorous invitations without reflecting upon it, so she carries on the role of 'intellectual' but refuses to reflect upon it. She skilfully presses the conversation in the direction of 'lofty' topics of conversation. But we may assume that, unless she is exceptionally skilful in this role, there will be a certain artificiality, a certain glib irrelevance about her conversation. There may even be momentary eruptions of patently flirtatious phrasing, expression, or gesture. Though Sartre himself has nothing to say about her role-playing other than that she does play a role, we can now see that the role-playing is not an expression of the Self, (the person) but is carried on in isolation as a discreet 'act', as a 'performance'. For example, she may say, 'I respect Camus' integrity', but this is a line appropriate to a role she has learned to play; it is not an expression of her respect for Camus' integrity—which may be non-existent. The observer sees her conversation as 'shallow'—but in a way sincere, not pure pretence.

Sartre emphasizes the 'transparency' of consciousness to itself. When he does treat the opacities within consciousness, mainly by use of his doctrine of 'impure reflection', he phrases the issues in terms of the denial of freedom and of transcendence, rather than as I have, in terms of the refusal to reflect on certain regions of Consciousness. Nevertheless, there can be no question that the refusal to reflect is a possibility inherent in Sartre's ontology of consciousness, though he himself never makes this possibility explicit or capitalizes on it. A consciousness which was unselective and reflected upon itself in its totality would consist of an infinite hierarchy of reflections of reflections, a condition Sartre grants to be self-evidently impossible.

The denial by reflective consciousness of freedom is not, as Sartre holds, the root of self-deception; the denial of freedom is the outcome of the refusal to reflect upon the disavowed project, and, as a consequence, the refusal to reflect upon the possibilities associated with that project. To put it another way, the denial of freedom in bad faith is the outcome of establishing a Self (by means of impure reflection) which excludes the project in question.

In Sartrian terms (but following our own reformulation), the core of self-deception is the disavowal of responsibility for, and the consequent refusal to reflect upon, some project of Consciousness.

Sartre, as we noted earlier, says that one 'puts oneself into *mauvaise foi* as one puts oneself to sleep'; it is a 'spontaneous determination of our being'. The alternative account I have given allows us to be much more specific and informative about this within the framework of Sartre's basic approach and terminology. This 'spontaneous determination' is a pre-reflective choice which we refuse to reflect upon, a refusal which obliges us not to reflect upon it in turn. Indeed this is like falling asleep in one crucial respect. For in going to sleep we to some extent *do* something, but we are unable to reflect upon what we are doing, for to reflect upon the fact that one is waiting for sleep is to hinder its coming. When one puts oneself to sleep one acts with purpose, but part of the skill consists finally in avoiding reflection upon one's purpose. One may even speculate that the analogy between putting oneself into *mauvaise foi* and putting oneself to sleep goes deeper. In both there is a purposeful alienation of the self from concerns which might normally be those of the self. In *mauvaise foi* the discrepancy between a particular concern and the totality of the person's concern is too great; the particular concern is alienated from the rest. In going to sleep, it is the totality of concerns which are given up temporarily. If one is *too* concerned, one's mind 'races' and one can't get to sleep. Sleep, in this perspective, appears as a normal, periodic disavowal of personal existence; it is a voluntary 'little death'.

Of course the analogy between sleep and *mauvaise foi* is not perfect. There is a critical element, in the case of sleep, which is independent of purpose and skill. To put oneself to sleep is to put oneself in a state in which, independently of further purposeful control, certain bodily reactions take place. But to put oneself in *mauvaise foi* one does not need to wait at a certain point for something analogous to *happen*. *Mauvaise foi* seems to have 'happened' only for the memory of reflective consciousness, which purposely averts its gaze at the time and therefore, later on, may report what did take place as if it were something which had 'happened' behind one's own back. It is this standpoint which is readily reflected in philosophical discussion, since philosophical discussion tends to begin with the deliverances of reflective consciousness. Thus philosophical discussions of self-deception tend naturally to lose sight of the voluntaristic aspect of it.

2. *Kierkegaard and Double-Mindedness*

Sartre's doctrine of self-deception is presented in a relatively systematic form and within the context of a single large work, *Being and Nothingness*. For this reason it lends itself to a critique which can be both systematic and relatively concise. Any comparable attempt in connection with Kierkegaard's views on self-deception is out of the question. Nevertheless, I think we can profit from some rather more discursive remarks concerning Kierkegaard.

Kierkegaard says (in *The Sickness Unto Death*) that man is a synthesis which is a relation between the temporal and the eternal, between freedom (or possibility) and necessity, between body and soul. But this synthesis, which is man, is not yet as such a self. The self is spirit. The synthesis of which Kierkegaard speaks, however, corresponds to what I have called an individual, the human being who has already reached the level of intelligent, purposeful action, but who is not yet a person. Kierkegaard compares the capacities at this level with those of the higher animals (*Either/Or*, p. 183)—as I have done in my own earlier remarks on the isolated forms of engagement characteristic of the individual as such.

The self, spirit, is for Kierkegaard an achievement, and the establishment of the self presents itself as a task for man. In the succinct but notably obscure statement at the outset of *The Sickness Unto Death*, Kierkegaard says, 'The self is a relation which relates itself to its own self. . . . The self is not the relation but consists in the fact that the relation relates itself to its own self' (p. 146).

We have an idea of what Kierkegaard means by the first relation mentioned in his formula—it is man as synthesis of body and soul. But what is this second relation, the relation generated when this first relation relates itself to its own self? What sort of relating to itself is this which establishes spirit? Since I have argued in Chapter Four that being a person is an achievement and is something over and above being an individual, it is appropriate for us to inquire whether the 'relation relating to its own self' has any similarity in meaning to what I have spoken of as the 'identification', 'avowal', or 'acknowledgment' which establishes the person.

Certainly the aspect of unity is of the essence of Kierkegaard's view of the self, as it is of mine. 'For he who is not himself a unity is never really anything wholly and decisively; he exists only in an external sense—as long as he lives as a numeral within the crowd. . . .' (*Purity*, p 184). Such a one is unable truly to 'will one thing', to keep free of 'double-mindedness', to avoid the 'inner psychical disagreement' in which lies 'the germs of double-mindedness' (*Purity*, p. 117).

The nature of this unity which is self or spirit is described by Kierkegaard in terms which could as readily have been used in expounding the doctrine of the person presented by me in Chapter Four. Kierkegaard, speaking of the self (what I have spoken of as the person), says

He (the self) has himself . . . as a task, in such a sort that the task is principally to order, cultivate, temper, enkindle, repress, in short to bring about a proportionality in the soul, a harmony, which is the fruit of the personal virtues.
(*Either/Or*, p. 267)

This harmony is not one whose elements can be selected at will or whim. The self is a kind of destiny in that it is a personal identity whose elements are given by the non-personal, by history and by the life of the individual. In my own terms, the person is not a creation *de novo*, but an avowal of the individual as in fact historically given, an avowal which establishes the multifariousness of the individual in a new harmony, in the unity of a personal identity which is accepted as such by itself.

The individual thus becomes conscious of himself as this definite individual, with these talents, these dispositions, these instincts, these passions, influenced by these definite surroundings, as this definite product of a definite environment. But being conscious of himself in this way, he assumes responsibility for all this. He does not hesitate as to whether he shall include this particular trait or the other, for he knows that he stands to lose something much higher if he does not. Thus, at the instant of choice he is in the most complete isolation . . . and yet at the same moment he is in absolute continuity, for he chooses himself as product. . . .

(Either/Or, p. 255)

We have already referred to Kierkegaardian language in which the element of will and of choice is stressed in connection with the establishment of this unity which is the self. Kierkegaard constantly refers to the 'task' of 'choosing one's self'. Kierkegaard is explicitly aware that it is natural to speak of this unity in terms of knowledge and ignorance; he often does so himself. But he is equally emphatic and explicit in his view of what lies at the heart of this 'knowledge':

The ethical individual knows himself, but this knowledge is not a mere contemplation. . . , it is a reflection upon himself which itself is an action, and therefore I have deliberately preferred to use the expression 'choose oneself' instead of know oneself.

(Either/Or, p. 263)

Thus, for Kierkegaard, the relation relating to its own self is the establishing of a kind of unity, through a will-like, or choice-like movement, in which the dis-

parate engagements of the historically given individual
are taken up out of their particularistic immediacy,
their 'aesthetic' movement towards mere gratification,
and transformed by integration into the unity of the
self. This movement, which is the founding of spirit,
is an 'ethical choice', says Kierkegaard. It is, he says,
the choice of good-and-evil as against the life of immediacy. Thus the founding of spirit is the establishment of the ethical agent. Or, to put the matter in
slightly different language to which we shall recur in
the final chapter of this book: To choose oneself as
an ethical agent is in itself a *spiritual* act, and only
prospectively an ethical act. It is this distinction between the spiritual and the ethical act which is abandoned by Sartre. Sartre sees the total acceptance of responsibility for oneself (roughly: avowal by the person
of the entire individual) as the realization of the ideal.
But Kierkegaard makes a distinction when he speaks
of the choice of the self as the choice of good-and-evil.
For the latter phrasing implies that the choice of the
self is the acceptance of moral responsibility but not
necessarily the choice of the *good*. To choose the self
is to become a moral agent—who then may choose
evil. Kierkegaard is not clear or explicit about the implications of this distinction. It often seems that in
practice he presumes the choice of the self amounts
to the willing of the *Good*; and this almost seems to
be necessarily his point in *Purity of Heart*.

I believe there is a distinction to be made here which
neither Sartre nor Kierkegaard clearly sees, a distinction I shall expand upon in the last chapter. The distinction is that between the person's acknowledging his
engagements *as* his, and his accepting responsibility
for those engagements. Since Sartre abandons all doctrinal reliance on the notion of 'objective' values,

acceptance of oneself is the only 'value' left for him. It is acceptance of responsibility in the fullest sense of that word. But Kierkegaard holds to the objective value of the Good, of God. Hence he always has in mind, though he may not always bring it out clearly or explicitly, that the unity in the acceptance of self is *per se* incomplete, that it is the religious dimension in which it is completed, in the relation of the one individual facing the one, eternal God.

After the preceding remarks, it will be relatively easy to see how Kierkegaard will develop his doctrine of despair, which is failure in the 'task', and sin, which is the despair of the Christian even in the face of Revelation.

Despair—not willing to be oneself—has various forms. One of them we shall not be able to discuss directly until later. But several forms are evident. Someone may be more or less ignorant of the possibility of this task, and thus he may embrace this life of immediacy and even suppose that he is single-minded and dedicated to some one thing. But what he calls one thing is not *the* One, the eternal, the Good, but it is some particular engagement; the pursuit of the latter inevitably has a changing career in the course of time and circumstance. Thus honesty must finally reveal that it is *not* truly '*one* thing'. Or, insofar as a man apprehends his task as that of choosing himself—and who does not in some degree apprehend this task?— he may be sufficiently clever to evade wholehearted commitment.

Alas there is in every man a power, a dangerous and at the same time a great power. This power is cleverness. . . . Now in the inner world man uses cleverness in a ruinous way, in order to keep himself from coming to a decision.

In countless ways cleverness can be so misused; . . . we will . . . simply designate this misuse by a definite expression: to seek to evade.

(Either/Or, p. 127)

The consequence of this evasion—of this disavowal —is, of course, that a danger is indeed avoided, as Kierkegaard says, but when this 'security' in double-mindedness is achieved, '. . . just at that point he has sunk into perdition' *(Either/Or,* p. 127). This perdition is the double-mindedness inherent in despair at not willing to be oneself. It is not to will the ethical life. Ultimately, in Kierkegaard's view, it is also not to will the foundation of the authentic religious life—for it is only as what Kierkegaard calls 'the individual' (what I have termed 'the person') that the saving relation to God can be achieved.

Although the theological aspects of Kierkegaard's thought are not of primary interest to us here, there are certain features of his doctrine of self and of self-deception which call for discussion of at least a 'de-mythologized' version of his theology. Kierkegaard's spokesman in *Either/Or,* Judge William, says, 'I am . . . born by the fact that I choose myself' *(Either/Or,* p. 220). But in the same place he also says, 'I am born of the principle of contradiction. . . .' The 'contradiction' in this choice is brought out when Kierkegaard asks, in *Sickness,* whether the self 'constituted itself' or has 'been constituted by another' (p. 146). It will repay us to consider this problem which is posed in such abstruse terms by Kierkegaard. For it concerns the conditions under which we can realize our personhood, or abandon it in self-deception.

Kierkegaard's view is that the self must be a 'derived', 'constituted' relation, not one which 'constitutes itself'. Thus there is a 'third term', a Power which constitutes the self, in addition to the first term (the synthesis) and the second term (the self). Why must there be a Power which constitutes the self?

We cannot suppose the person to constitute himself. The person could not pre-exist himself; he could not exist first, and then afterwards make avowals, identifications, and thus bring himself into existence as a personal identity. This would be not paradox but nonsense. The person is constituted by avowal, and if there are not yet avowals, there is not yet a person. On the other hand, we cannot suppose that there are avowals *prior* to the existence of the person, these avowals ultimately bringing the person into being—for avowals are avowals *of* the person.

Let us consider this latter point further. Judge William says that the essential task is to choose the absolute and to do so absolutely—'and what is the absolute? It is I myself in my eternal validity' (*Either/Or*, p. 218). When Kierkegaard speaks of choosing the self as an absolute choice, a very important part of what he means is that the self is not a particular object chosen by (avowed by) a self, nor is the self a particular experience of a self. The self is that *for* which there are many particular experiences. The self persists through the flux of experience and action; it is the identity, the unity in the variety, and this is essential to its character. The self is eternal, says Kierkegaard, though it participates in the flux of the temporal. The self is therefore not something which comes into existence *after* the choice, *after* avowals. It is not created by our choice, says Kierkegaard.

This way of putting the matter—that the self could not pre-exist itself and therefore *comes into existence* (is 'born') by the fact that I choose myself, and yet that the self must already (eternally) *exist* in order to be chosen and in order to do the 'choosing'—leads Kierkegaard to speak of the self as 'born of the principle of contradiction' (*Either/Or*, p. 220). But we can formulate the same point somewhat less paradoxically. Granted that the 'choosing of the self' is not choice in an ordinary sense, but 'in an absolute sense', we may reasonably argue that Kierkegaard emphasizes the paradox precisely as a way of emphasizing that we are not dealing here with the usual situation in which an already existent self chooses an object or a course of conduct. Instead we are dealing with the emergence of the self, and we are simultaneously stressing that the self has as its essence a peculiar internal relation which we can express by saying that it acknowledges itself as an identity, as a person. Thus it is logically impossible that there was a *time* when the person existed which was prior to his acknowledging himself as a person; or that there was a time when the acknowledgment existed prior to his existence as a person. The air of paradox enters because the description of the emergence of the self is cast in terms of 'choice', of 'willing oneself', and in ordinary contexts this does imply certain temporal relations and a certain logical independence between the person who chooses or wills and that which is chosen or willed. The paradox is introduced when we adopt the language of choice in which to talk about this emergence of the self. Yet the important constructive insights of Kierkegaard in this matter derive precisely from his use of this language to emphasize certain features of the entire situation. Those features are the ones I have tried to isolate by use of 'avow', 'acknowledge', and 'identify oneself as'.

The self does emerge. What 'power' brings it about? Having rejected as unintelligible the individual or a pre-existent self as the 'power' which brings this about, we are led to what Kierkegaard calls the 'third term', the Power which does bring it about. We may expatiate upon this Power in theological terms, as Kierkegaard does, or we may, for the time being, merely say that the world is such as to bring it about that individuals do become persons; this is an issue we need not debate here. We need only add that, on either view, the self is, as Kierkegaard says, grounded 'transparently' in that Power which posited it. For, by 'transparent' I believe he means that whatever the nature of that grounding Power, its grounding role in no way whatsoever vitiates the fact that a self has the identity that it has *entirely* by virtue of its *own* acknowledgment of itself as itself. What the person disavows (disidentifies himself with) is indeed not himself (though the individual may continue in the engagement). In Kierkegaard's language: '. . . only that belongs to me essentially which I ethically (i.e., as a person) accept as my task. If I refuse to accept it, then what belongs to me is that I have refused it' (*Either/Or,* p. 265). It is this entire coincidence of the content of the self with what it acknowledges as itself that reveals what Kierkegaard means when he speaks of the self as freely and absolutely 'willed' or 'chosen', as grounded *transparently* in the Power which posits it.

On the other hand, it is the necessity for a Power to constitute the self, it is the self's incapacity to constitute itself which calls for a profound humility with respect to our task. Indeed, it is the evasion of this recognition and this humility which constitutes the main form of despair we have not yet discussed—'despairingly willing to be oneself'. This is the despair of *hubris*, as it were; it is the despair of trying to carry out the task entirely as an act of personal will.

Despair is eradicated, says Kierkegaard, when two conditions are fulfilled: (1) one takes up the task of willing to be oneself, (the 'relation relating itself to its own self'); and, (2) the self is 'grounded transparently' in the 'Power which constituted it'. We can paraphrase this, in the language of Chapter Four, by saying: Self-deception is resolved when the disavowed engagement of the individual is avowed; authentic avowal must be understood as a peculiarly personal and unique manoeuvre which is not subject like ordinary actions to the natural contingency of the immediate time and circumstance of the action, nor is it an 'act of will' or 'choice' in the ordinary sense of these phrases, though avowal has features akin to action, will, and choice.

We can tie together the Kierkegaardian themes which we have now discussed: Purity of heart is to will one thing and to will it absolutely—it is the self as the unity of the entire individual acknowledged as self; it is thus the founding of the eternal, of that which endures through change and even within change; it is the condition of the truly ethical life, and ultimately of the truly saving religious life. Insofar as the person fails ever to avow, or disavows his individual engagements, he is to that extent immersed in the particular and immediate, has abdicated the harmonious unity and synthesis of the ethical, and is in despair. It is in the nature of despair that it is double-mindedness. Whether we view the self-deceiver as inwardly evasive in a clever way towards himself, or whether we view him externally as nothing but engagement in the temporal, the particular, the immediate, there is a fundamental multipleness in his existence. In either case, he is seen as the victim, within time, of particularity, rather than as the eternal surveyor of time and multiplicity.

CHAPTER SIX

EGO AND COUNTER-EGO

I find myself for a moment in the interesting position of not knowing whether what I have to say should be regarded as something long familiar and obvious or as something entirely new and puzzling. But I am inclined to think the latter.

I have at last been struck by the fact that . . .

(*23*, 275)

THESE are the provocative opening words in Freud's last paper, unfinished and posthumously published under the title, 'The Splitting of the Ego in the Process of Defence.' Freud's opening remark is all the more provocative because he had just previously made two attempts, both left incomplete by him, to present a definitive restatement of psychoanalytic theory. With these uncompleted efforts in the immediate background, he turned to 'The Splitting of the Ego . . .' and one naturally suspects that the provocative opening words of this last short paper may announce some fundamental new insight which he had been struggling to assimilate.

On its face, this last paper is merely a brief restatement of material quite familiar from discussions in a number of Freud's writings. These discussions go as far back as the early writings; they are found from time to time in later papers; and they constitute an unusually large proportionate part of the highly condensed *Outline of Psychoanalysis*, on which he had been working only a few months prior.

That the material in 'The Splitting of the Ego . . .' should look familiar to us is to be expected, since Freud himself introduces it as having a 'long familiar and obvious' look. What was there about it, then, that was 'entirely new and puzzling'? It must have been a *way* of seeing the familiar 'fact' by which he was now 'struck' anew.

I believe that what struck Freud was a central insight analogous to that which I have developed in earlier chapters of this book. He saw a new way of generalizing the role of the ego in defence, a way which for the first time could bring into focus certain fundamental implications of his entire theory, a way which had the potential for resolving certain deep conceptual problems internal to his theory. Freud did not live to develop the potential of this new insight. Some aspects of it have in effect been central to very recent theoretical discussions of defence and the unconscious in the psychoanalytic literature. But these discussions have still failed to expose the central, unifying element in Freud's insight because they are basically cast in the old terms.

I propose to review briefly here some of the fundamental conceptual problems internal to psychoanalytic theory which call for the solution Freud finally proposed. Such a critique is necessary if we are to appreciate the significance of his new proposals. For an important element in the entire affair is to formulate or to press questions which have remained hitherto unformulated or, by and large, ignored.

Some Fundamental Questions Concerning Defence

The first of the specific problems internal to psycho-analytic theory with which we shall take up the discussion is an old one. It was long ago identified and partly resolved by Freud, and it was then lost from sight until very recently.

Defence is unconscious: although the clinical data forced this fact upon Freud, his earlier theory was in-consistent with it. The earlier versions of his theory postulated conflict between what is unconscious and what is conscious; defence was viewed as a positive effort by consciousness aimed at keeping unconscious something which strives towards consciousness. Yet in clinical work Freud saw that the patient is not conscious that he is engaged in defence; moreover the patient actively resists becoming conscious of the defence as well as that which he is defending himself against. Thus what is defined by theory as an activity of con-sciousness turns out in the clinic to have the typical marks of the unconscious: it is phenomenologically not conscious, and there is persistent effort to keep it so.

It is well known how Freud at last proposed funda-mental elaborations of his theory in order to resolve this difficulty (along with certain others which do not concern us here and which I shall simply pass by in silence). Consciousness was no longer postulated to be an essential feature of the defending agency. The latter was now called by Freud the ego, a term he had earlier used loosely but to which he now proceeded to give a specific, technical sense. He characterized the ego as an agency which is in part conscious (or pre-conscious), and also in part unconscious. Conscious-ness is now a 'quality' which may or may not belong to certain of the ego functions. In accordance with the clinical data, defensive manoeuvres are characterized as unconscious ego manoeuvres. The earlier inconsistency between theory and fact is removed.

A contradiction was removed—yet this was by no means equivalent to providing a specific, intelligible account of the unconsciousness of defence. The problem as Freud left it, and as it in my opinion still exists, may be expressed in the form of two closely related sets of questions.

(1) If it is the ego which regulates defence, which, for example, represses an id derivative, *how* does it keep itself unconscious of what it is doing? Is its defensive activity *dynamically* unconscious, i.e., itself the object of defence? But then how shall we account for this latter defensive manoeuvre, i.e., the 'second-level' manoeuvre of keeping from consciousness the initial defensive manoeuvre? Is this 'second-level' defensive manoeuvre available to consciousness, or is it in turn dynamically unconscious because, for example, repressed by still a third level of repressive defence? Then somewhere, finally, we must come to grips with the problem of the last term in this hierarchy. Is the last defence in the hierarchy conscious (or readily available to consciousness)? The only alternative to an infinite regress would seem to be to suppose that the defence—or at least the last defence in such a hierarchy—is *not* dynamically unconscious. How, then, shall we account for that resistance to the uncovering of defence which is actually found in therapy? We are back to the original problem: How can the ego resist itself, hide from itself? This problem was energetically pressed by Sartre, but it has received very little attention in the psychoanalytic literature.

The second set of questions concerns not *how* the

ego keeps defences unconscious, but *why*. Indeed the question is broader than this: why should the ego aim to keep anything at all unconscious, whether it be defence or impulse? This, which I take to be the more fundamental problem at the core of psychoanalytic theory, has so far as I know been raised neither by psychoanalysts nor by contemporary philosophical reinterpreters of Freud such as Sartre or, more recently, Ricoeur. The question bears elaboration.

Let us suppose that the defensive rejection of an impulse is designed not merely to inhibit its expression but characteristically to 'hide' its existence. But from whom or what is the impulse to be hidden? Other persons in the environment? If this were all, it would merely be a case of ordinary deception, whereas what is characteristic of defence is that one 'hides' something from *oneself*. But where shall we locate the inner 'victim' of this secretiveness? Is the impulse to be hidden from the id? This makes no sense, for it is the impulse *of* the id. Is it to be hidden from the superego? No, for it is typically the superego which perceives the emerging id derivatives, and which typically initiates the defence by inducing anxiety in the ego. Is the impulse to be hidden from the ego? Surely not, for the ego is by definition that 'agency' which takes into account *both* the impulse and the conflicting superego demands, and which then designs and executes the defensive manoeuvre. Furthermore since the impulse remains active in the id, defence is a continuing process; the ego must therefore remain *continuously* cognizant of all relevant factors if defence is to succeed. However, if nothing relevant is 'hidden' from id, ego, or superego, what is the point of keeping anything from being conscious? We can no longer assume it to be—as is usually assumed—some kind of hiding of the impulse from oneself, some kind of ignorance due to successful 'disguise'. The plausibility of assigning importance to consciousness has typically derived from use of this word to suggest or even to imply knowledge. As we have noted in earlier chapters, this assimilation of ideas is encouraged by such transitional terms as 'awareness', or such bridging metaphors as 'see'. However in the present case the imputation of knowledge to consciousness, and ignorance to unconsciousness, seems to have lost its justification.

The thesis that the concept of consciousness lacks further interest for psychoanalytic theory has been argued in very recent years by some of the leading theoreticians among relatively orthodox psychoanalysts. We shall discuss these views shortly. These writers have not appreciated, however, that the relegation of the question of consciousness from the centre to the periphery of psychoanalytic attention leaves all the more acute the question as to how defence serves the purpose that theory presumes it to serve. Defence aims to reduce anxiety, of course, and so long as the main outcome of defence was thought to be a form of self-induced ignorance, it made a certain sense to suppose that 'what you don't know won't worry you'. But once we abandon the notion that defence brings a kind of blissful ignorance to some 'agency' of the mind, the question forces itself upon one: why should anxiety be reduced by defence any more than, better than, or differently than would be the case if we merely curbed our impulses and/or deceived others quite consciously?

Nor can we be quite so ready to abandon the notion of consciousness in psychoanalytic theory: after all, why is so much effort expended by psychoanalytic therapists—even those who now minimize the significance of consciousness—to impart insight at the right moment?

All these questions require detailed discussion.

How The Ego Keeps Its Defences Unconscious

With respect to the first set of questions, in which the issue is not *why* but *how* defence is kept unconscious, there have been, at last, several recent attempts to resolve the problem. Gill is one of those who has for this purpose elaborated on the view of Rapaport and others that the defence is kept from consciousness by being in turn the object of further ego defence. Gill maintains that the series of defences against defences form a 'hierarchy' of defences which may be of great complexity (pp. 98ff.). The inevitable problem— avoidance of the implication of infinite regress—is handled by Gill in a way which is suggestive, yet unfortunately too vague and ambiguous to disclose the important issues here. He argues that there is always in each series of defences against defences a last term: a 'specific content which is able to attain consciousness, and though it serves defensive purposes is not *recognized* as a defence' (italics in original, p. 98).

The phrase on which Gill's entire proposal rests is: 'not recognized as'. It is a phrase with no technical status, and it is crucially ambiguous. Presumably Gill here means that the 'defensive purpose' is in some way not conscious. We must ask: Is it unconscious because of defence (i.e., is it dynamically unconscious), or is it merely not conscious but readily available to consciousness (i.e., preconscious)? It is on exactly this distinction that the problem turns. If 'not recognized' means 'preconscious', then the hypothesis amounts to saying that the 'defensive *purpose*' is preconscious; and Gill has already said that the 'defensive *content*' is 'able to attain consciousness', i.e., is preconscious. In short, on this interpretation both content and purpose are preconscious. This interpretation is implausible if only because, assuming it to be his meaning, there would have been no reason to contrast defensive content and defensive purpose as he does in his formula.

On the other hand, if 'not recognized' means—as it surely must mean if it is to fit the clinical data—not conscious due to some *resistance* to making it conscious, then we are back to the infinite regress which the proposal was designed to avoid: whence comes this resistance to 'recognizing' the defensive purpose; and what keeps it, in turn, unconscious?

It is plain that we get no further in solving our problem by inserting a hierarchy of defences, but we shall later see that Gill's distinction in this context between the content of the defence and the purpose of the defence can be a helpful one here. And it may be remarked at once that it amounts, in substance, to the point made in an earlier chapter concerning the overt playing of a role (the conscious content) while disavowing the role-playing conduct (unconscious purpose). Thus our earlier conceptual analysis is supported by Gill's clinical and theoretical insight. But, for lack of a coherent psychoanalytic doctrine of defence, his theoretical formulation remains ambiguous and incomplete.

The chief alternative to the type of view held by Gill is that proposed by Eissler. The latter argues to the effect that we have a pseudo-problem, that we need not account for how defences become unconscious. For, says Eissler, defences don't *become* unconscious since they are inherently non-conscious. Eissler uses a key analogy: we are not conscious of the process by which an image on our retina is transformed and 'projected' into the external world; we are conscious only of the result, of the object as finally seen located in space. Analogously, a defence-generated symptom emerges in consciousness, but the ego has no more need to take special steps to keep the defensive process unconscious than it has in the case of visual processes. Both the defensive process and the visual projection process are in their very nature not conscious; they are not 'dynamically unconscious' (pp. 34ff.).

While it is of course true that the visual processes mentioned by Eissler are inherently non-conscious, this is not entirely so with respect to defence. Indeed, what is distinctive about defence is that in certain crucial respects it bears the marks of the dynamically unconscious: in certain respects it *can* become conscious, but we resist consciousness of it. We need only recall that it is dynamic insight into the defences which has long been associated by psychoanalysts with a movement towards health. Whatever the reasons, good or bad, for this supposition, it would have been unintelligible if what is referred to as 'defence' were necessarily and totally non-conscious. Eissler has clearly evaded the problem by allowing himself to concentrate his attention on the tempting analogies between vision and defence, while losing sight of the lack of analogy in certain critical respects.

Before beginning our own constructive account of how defence can be unconscious, let us note that for present purposes there is no theoretical problem about how the repressed *impulse* is kept for consciousness. According to standard doctrine, the ego withholds a hypercathexis (i.e., the specific attention-cathexis which establishes a mental content as explicitly conscious).

In addition, the ego directs a counter-cathexis on to the ideational derivatives of the impulse, thus removing them from status as preconscious (i.e., from the status of being available for attention hypercathexis). The impulse is now dynamically unconscious. (We shall ignore the complicating factor of id-cathexes for the time being, since it is not relevant to our immediate problem.)

The crucial question for us, of course, concerns not the means by which the impulse is kept unconscious but the means by which the defensive activity itself is kept unconscious. The answer to this question lies in turning our question upside down. Instead of asking how the defensive action is kept unconscious, we need to ask how it—or *any* mental content—ever is made to be conscious. Instead of being puzzled by a mental content's not being conscious, we must become puzzled a bit by its becoming conscious.

The question as typically formulated rests on a concern with the counter-cathexis, the relatively exceptional, special manoeuvre by which the ego defends itself against what is radically alien to it. Psychoanalysts have tended to overlook the significance of the fact that the mere absence of counter-cathexis is not enough to make something explicitly conscious, though it allows it to be preconscious. The ego has a further task if it is to make an ego activity (or indeed any *mental* activity) explicitly conscious. As we have already noted, psychoanalytic theory postulates an additional cathexis, an 'attention hypercathexis', if anything is to be made explicitly conscious. To say a mental element is *pre*conscious is to say, among other things, that it satisfies all the conditions for being conscious except one—it is not hypercathected.

I am not concerned here with the many problems

generated by the much debated theoretical concept of cathexis. What is crucial to my argument is the psychoanalytic postulate that becoming explicitly conscious requires a quite specific 'mental act', an act in which the ego selects a particular item from an indefinitely large range of possible items, and highlights this particular item. Can we say anything more about the nature of this act?

I have shown in detail elsewhere (*Self in Transformation*, Ch. 1) that, whatever the other changes in his theoretical views over the years, Freud always was convinced that language was the essence, or very intimately related to the essence, of preconsciousness and consciousness. This strongly suggests, though Freud never put it this way, that the 'mental act' denoted by 'hypercathexis' is essentially a kind of linguistic or paralinguistic act. It is, I suggest, much the same as what I have called 'spelling-out'. I think it reasonable to say that preconsciousness is the state of being available for spelling-out on particular appropriate occasions, and that Freud means by 'conscious' what I have called 'explicit consciousness'.

The ego does not hypercathect at random or in some automatic way; it hypercathects when there is reason to do so—and of course it will *not* hypercathect when (a) there is no reason to do so, or (b) there is overriding reason not to do so. The latter consideration is relevant in the case of defence. For a defensive counter-cathexis (which corresponds, as we shall see, with what I call disavowal) amounts to a removal, as a matter of 'policy', of some mental content from the status of being available to hypercathexis, i.e., spelling-out.

It is time now to sort out briefly various aspects of what psychoanalysts call 'defence'. This will not only enable us to distinguish those aspects which are inherently nonconscious from those which are capable of being conscious, but it will remove critical vagueness which handicaps from the start the attempts of Gill and Eissler.

In speaking of 'the defences' one sometimes has in mind the *forms* of defence (the types of 'defence mechanisms'), e.g., repression, projection, reaction formation. These are classifications within psychological doctrine, not immediate data of a subject's consciousness. There are also, as already noted, the hypothesized '*processes*' of defence, the shifts in cathexes. This is an explanatory model, never an immediate datum in consciousness, and it is in this connection that we deal with what is sound in Eissler's theses.

'Defence' is also used with reference to the *content* of the defence. For example, the content of the reaction-formation defence against aggressive impulses would, of course, be an excessive and inflexible 'affectionate-ness' of manner, an 'affectionateness' which is not rooted in, or at least not entirely rooted in genuinely affectionate impulses. We need now to make a distinction that is not usually made here. This content may *become* conscious, but so long as the defence is effective, it remains nonconscious, not hypercathected. In his role as one who is affectionate, the defensively 'affectionate' person says and does the things at least superficially characteristic of a genuinely affectionate person. The latter is or can readily become conscious of his affection. But it is erroneous to say, as Gill does, that defensive content can become conscious even while remaining the content of defence. A tacit awareness of this point is often reflected in informal comment to the effect that the defensive person doesn't 'see' his pseudo-affectionateness as it 'really' is; he cannot express to himself or others what to us are the distinctive elements of his comportment. He says, 'I was cordial, wasn't I?' We would say he was annoyingly effusive. If he attains insight into his defence in the course of therapy, he seems to 'see' it for the first time. Then he can say—with complete conceptual propriety—that he never really felt the affection he had claimed. For he now appreciates, in effect, that his claims of affection were *not ever* expressions of what he was feeling; they were gestures belonging to a role he was not explicitly conscious he was playing. Even his 'explicit' protestations when challenged—'But I *do* feel very affectionate towards Aunt Martha'—were not expressions of the 'content of consciousness' but the required gestures of one who plays the role of affectionate nephew. We register this tacitly when we sense the artificiality of his protestation, even as we grant that in a way he is sincere, not uttering a barefaced lie. If we say he is confused about his own feelings, we mean, in effect, that he purposefully does not spell-out to himself or others the feelings he has.

In speaking of defence we often refer to the *specific aim* of the defence; for example the aim would be to inhibit and/or camouflage an aggressive impulse towards a parent-figure. Our aims, of course, can in general become conscious (be hypercathected). In the case of defence, however, there is resistance to becoming conscious of the aim; the ego carefully avoids hypercathecting it.

There is, finally, the generic *motive* for defence, anxiety. Anxiety may also, in general, become conscious, though typically consciousness of the motive for defence is resisted.

We have by no means exhausted all aspects of defence, but the preceding will serve as a basis for stating explicitly, within the framework of current theory, and more completely than we have been able to do until now, how it is that defence is kept from consciousness.

The aim of inhibiting the expression of an aggressive impulse is the kind of thing which in general can become conscious. When this is the aim of defence, there is a peculiar difficulty: to hypercathect the aim would be to hypercathect the aggressive impulse as well, for the aggressive impulse is an essential constituent of the content of the aim. But if we assume there is defence, we are assuming the aggressive impulse has been counter-cathected; thus it now is in a status which precludes hypercathexis. Thus, in turn, the aim of inhibiting the impulse is perforce excluded from hypercathexis, too. Much the same kind of argument holds with regard to the motive of defence: to hypercathect the anxiety *as due to the aggressive impulse* is of course to hypercathect the impulse. But this, as already remarked, is excluded. At most the ego may hypercathect the anxiety *per se*. But of course the anxiety will then be perceived either as free-floating anxiety or as attached (displaced) to some other datum of consciousness.

Thus, to summarize, given a counter-cathexis of the impulse, the entire dynamic complex is excluded from consciousness—a theoretical conclusion which exactly conforms with clinical fact. This conclusion also is parallel to the account I have given of the automatically self-covering aspect of the policy not to spell something out.

The Splitting of the Ego

We now have a coherent theory as to how both impulse and defence do not reach consciousness. The surprising question which now faces us is this: Why is absence from consciousness a defence? The discussion in section III strongly suggests that no important purpose can be served by keeping anything from consciousness. We assumed in Part III that the ego does defend itself in this way, but we cannot evade the fact that our detailed account, though showing the structure of defence, makes it seem puzzlingly pointless. The analysis up to this point confirms the necessity of raising the questions posed in the very first section of this chapter.

The question we now face is a surprising question because, after all, one of the earliest and most characteristic insights of psychoanalysis was that the origin of much psychopathology lies in the tactic of defending oneself from threats, inner or outer, by keeping oneself unconscious of them. This distinctive and illuminating insight has suddenly been transformed into a source of puzzlement and obscurity. Recent psychoanalytic theorists have argued, though not always for identical reasons, that the concepts of consciousness, preconsciousness, and unconsciousness play little or no essential role in contemporary theory. I believe they are wrong. However, even if they are right, the problem of the usefulness of defence would remain a central problem unresolved within psychoanalytic theory. The problem is not only unresolved, it is not even recognized by psychoanalytic theorists. Everyone has for long taken it for granted that defence serves a vital purpose; no one has appreciated that the purpose so long taken for granted, the *only* purpose postulated by theory, no longer is adequate to its theoretical burden.

Arlow and Brenner have been among the leading proponents of the thesis that psychoanalytic theory can get along without the use of the 'conscious-unconscious' cluster of concepts. They hold that in the work of the analyst, 'To characterize a mental element as accessible or inaccessible to consciousness does not tell us what we need to know' (p. 112).

There is much force in their detailed argument. Yet a healthy respect for the oldest and most characteristic of psychoanalytic insights in psychoanalysis might suggest caution. In fact the seeds of inner inconsistency are to be found in Arlow and Brenner's own exposition of their thesis.

For example, Arlow and Brenner present material from two different cases in which, in each instance, it is important to their commentary that certain interpretations, believed to be correct by the analyst, were nevertheless not presented to the patient at a certain time (pp. 106-9). To have presented these interpretations at that point, say Arlow and Brenner, would have been inappropriate, in one case perhaps dangerous. In thus acknowledging the critical therapeutic role of interpretation, Arlow and Brenner accept in practice what in theory they reject; for, what is interpretation if not the attempt to make explicitly conscious what was not conscious?

It will not help their case to argue that the newer aim of psychoanalysis is not so much 'to make the unconscious conscious' but rather to bring it about that 'where id was, there shall ego be'. We may readily grant the historical shift of emphasis expressed in these familiar slogans. The fact remains that therapeutic interpretation, aimed at dynamic insight, remains a principal analytic tool to achieve this newer aim. As such, interpretation—and thus the making conscious of what was unconscious—must remain of profound interest for both practice and theory. The Arlow and Brenner monograph, however, has little to say on therapy, nothing to say about the nature of dynamic insight. This is a predictable oversight in an argument designed to induce us to dispense with the conscious-unconscious distinction.

It seems that, at least in therapeutic practice, we cannot dismiss the question of the consciousness status of a mental content; but neither can we dismiss the more recent, theoretical lines of argument exemplified in the Arlow and Brenner monograph.

I propose, in summary, certain postulates which I believe must be accepted and which in fact are accepted in the solution which I shall present to this dilemma. These postulates derive, respectively, from the traditional psychoanalytic viewpoint, the newer Arlow-Brenner type of emphasis, and my own analysis of self-deception in earlier chapters.

(1) *The traditional element*: Defence is not merely the inhibition of discharge, for this in itself would amount only to self-control; defence characteristically has a self-alienating nature as well. Furthermore, this self-alienation in defence is characteristically reflected in an alteration of consciousness.

(2) *The Arlow-Brenner thesis*: What primarily counts in defence is the 'dynamic' aspect, not the presence or absence of some 'mental quality', i.e., some para-perceptual or cognitive element.

(3) *My own thesis*: The alteration of consciousness in defence should not be understood primarily in terms of knowledge and ignorance but, instead, by reference to the 'dynamics' of defence—that is, by reference to those features of defence which we would in everyday language refer to in such terms as 'purpose', 'will', 'motive', and, finally, 'action'.

It is fundamental to the solution I propose that one recalls how, from the very beginning, defence has been conceived psychoanalytically as the establishment of a kind of split in the psyche. Prior to the development of Freud's ego psychology, the split was conceived to be between the Conscious and the Unconscious, each eventually conceived as a system. By the 1920's, when the newer theses concerning anxiety and the ego-id-superego trio were developed, the split was conceived to be essentially between the ego (prodded by the super-ego) and the id. The two versions, however, retain a remarkable parallelism, a persistent cluster of insights, which is of special interest to us here. In both versions, the conflicting entities are conceived as systems which are quasi-autonomous, indeed incompatible, alienated from one another. One system contains what has been rejected by the other. The former system operates according to the 'archaic', 'primary process'; logical, temporal and causal relations are ignored, part stands for whole, isolated similarities establish equivalencies, and so on. The latter system operates to the more rational 'secondary process'. The two systems interact by way of conflict rather than co-ordination.

By virtue of the parallelism in these respects of the older and newer versions of the theory, neither system escapes certain problems. For example, unconscious fantasies are assigned in both the earlier and later versions of Freud's theory to the system which contains the repressed, the system which operates according to the primary process. As a matter of clinical fact, however, unconscious fantasies are found to be organized to a good extent according to the (rational) secondary process. Such paradoxes as this arise because both earlier and later versions are parallel in insisting correctly on the fact that there is a split in the psyche, but in failing to define the nature of the split adequately. In both versions, Freud *over*stressed the fact that the element split off from the Ego takes on a markedly 'primitive' character, and he fails adequately to stress the great extent to which the element split off still retains fundamental characteristics of the Ego (and superego).

If we correct this one-sidedness, the situation can be stated as follows. The result of defence is to split off from the more rational system (i.e., the system which is defended) a nuclear, dynamic complex. This nuclear entity is a complex of motive, purpose, feeling, perception, and drive towards action. It is, for example, an angry and competitive impulse to damage one's father as object of envy; or it may be an erotic and competitive impulse to arrange matters so as to be the adored son. And in such cases there is typically a sense of guilt as an element in the complex, the guilt being of a kind which is appropriate to a relatively infantile appreciation of the impulse and its expression. Also integral to such impulses is a limited but genuine capacity to adapt the expression of the impulse to varying reality situations.

Of course what we have been describing is a kind of split-off *ego*-structure. True, it is only a nucleus of an ego, split-off from the highly elaborated Ego. In relation to the Ego it is rudimentary in organization, especially with regard to the way it now fails to reflect the richness of the Ego's learning and many identifications. Isolated as it is from the learning and experimentation constantly engaged in by a healthy Ego, the split-off nucleus remains relatively static (and therefore relatively rudimentary) as compared to the continually maturing Ego. The longer it remains split-off, the greater the disparity between split-off nucleus and the Ego—and therefore the greater the tendency for it to remain split-off.

Why is such an ego-nucleus split-off from the Ego? It is because the incompatibility between the ego-nucleus and the current Ego are so great, relative to the integrative capacities of that Ego, that the latter gives up any attempt to integrate the ego-nucleus itself. The Ego then adopts some more or less sophisticated version of the *Ur*-defence postulated by Freud: so to speak, the Ego says, This is *not-me*. The Ego treats this unassimilable but still ego-like system as 'outside' rather than 'inside'.

This earliest defence of the infant against stress, as postulated by Freud, is in fact, I maintain, the model of all defence. This proposal is squarely in the spirit of Freud's theory-building, in which we find that it is a characteristic conceptual strategy to postulate the earliest form of any category of response as the model upon which later refinements and elaborations of that category of response are built.

The defensive outcome, then, is to establish what we may call a *counter-ego nucleus,* this nucleus being the structural aspect of counter-cathexis. The notion of the counter-ego nucleus is thus a generalization in 'structural' terms of the 'economic' concept of 'counter-cathexis'.

What I have said above constitutes, I believe, an account in essentially psychoanalytic language of facts known since Freud, though never before characterized in just this way. I have described these long familiar facts in such a way as to emphasize that the defensive process is a splitting of the ego which is not something that 'happens' to the ego but something the ego *does,* a motivated strategy. It is this which I believe at last 'struck' Freud and which furnished the central theme of his last paper, 'The Splitting of the Ego in the Process of Defence'. What Freud called the 'entirely new' yet 'long familiar and obvious' fact was that he was 'clearly at fault' to 'take for granted the synthetic (i.e., integrative) nature of the processes of the ego' (*23*, 276). For the ego has another major function which had always had a generic *name,* 'defence', but whose *character* as the exact complement of ego-synthesis had never been properly understood or appreciated. 'The defence mechanisms' had been the label on a basket into which a categorially mixed collection of items had been stored. It is true that the generic motive for defence—to reduce anxiety—was finally appreciated by Freud in the 1920s. However, the generic mode of operation, or even the fact that there is a generic mode of operation —the ego's splitting off from itself a counter-ego nucleus—was never appreciated by him until the very last days of his life. At that time, if I am right, he saw this clearly while in the course of a final review and restatement of the fundamentals of his theory.

Freud on a number of occasions used language close to that which I have used. He spoke of defence as 'disavowal' or a 'rejection' in the case of what was 'outer' or 'inner' respectively (*Outline, 23,* p. 204). He finally saw, I think, that the generic aim of defence is, in infantile oral terms, to 'spit out', or in the more everyday language which Freud used, to 'disavow' or 'reject'. This disavowal or rejection is the generic feature of defence, and it corresponds to what I have called disavowal in earlier chapters. The substance of the idea of a splitting of the ego is to be found rather clearly in his early writings. As on a number of other occasions in his career, Freud was in later life discovering anew, and in a far broader perspective, an idea which had been expressed explicitly by him very early. In the early *Studies in Hysteria,* he wrote in connection with defence :

When this process occurs for the first time there comes into being a nucleus and centre of crystallization for the formation of a psychical group divorced from the ego— a group around which everything which would imply an acceptance of the incompatible idea subsequently collects.

(2, 123)

The notion of a 'psychical group' was used with some frequency in the earlier writings of Freud (see 9, pp. 100-102), but this notion became assimilated to the word 'complex', which in turn came to be associated with certain of Jung's early ideas. The words no longer appear in Freud's writing after his estrangement from Jung; and the Freudian notion they express seems likewise to have dropped below the surface—always implied, as I have argued, but no longer explicit or properly appreciated. (However a doctrine of 'ego-nuclei' has been propounded for many years by the distinguished English psychoanalyst, Edward Glover.)

The preceding remarks lead us to see in a new way something of the nature of that resistance which Freud called the resistance of the id. A counter ego-nucleus, however rudimentary, has its own dynamism; it has that thrust towards its own aims which establishes it as ego-like rather than id. Herein is a source of that persistence which Freud ascribed to the id as repository of the repressed. Herein is also a source of what has been called the cathexes from the id which 'attract' additional material into the unconscious.

Psychoanalytic therapeutic technique is basically designed to offer to the counter-ego the possibility of some substantial gratification in altered form and harmoniously with the Ego, and to offer to the Ego the possibility of a bearable avowal of the counter-ego. The therapist thus makes possible avowal (removal of counter-cathexis and integration of the counter-ego into the ego).

The most markedly noticeable expression of avowal is usually associated with the new ability to hyper-cathect, i.e., the readiness of the patient to spell-out (not merely to 'intellectualize' about) the impulse which had been disavowed. Thus the patient's *explicit* acceptance of a therapeutic interpretation is a distinctive, but not a necessary condition, of the giving up of the defence. Or in still other words, dynamic insight, the becoming conscious of what was unconscious, is not the essence of dissolving the defence, nor is it the absolute aim of therapy, but it is a distinctive and natural expression of one's having abandoned defence. The 'dynamic' essence of defence is what I have called disavowal. This way of putting the matter, which follows from the theoretical critique I have presented, also is consistent with the traditional emphasis on explicit insight and with the newer emphasis by Arlow, Brenner, et al., on the dynamics of defence.

Though I have stressed the ego-like character of what is disavowed, this is by way of corrective compensation for the usual emphasis on its id-character. The rudimentary character of counter-ego nuclei, their isolation from the civilizing influence of the Ego, and the consequent lessening of concern with strict logical, causal, temporal, and other highly rational relationships, makes counter-ego nuclei much cruder, more 'primitive', in the form of their expression. They are indeed 'closer' to the id insofar as the latter constitutes the uncivilized, highly unspecific basic drives.

To conceive defence in terms of the metaphor of 'disavowal' rather than 'hiding' takes some re-thinking in contexts where the 'hiding' metaphor and the ignorance-knowledge schema dominate our use of 'conscious' and 'unconscious'. We are now in a position to specify those features of the situation in defence which justify the traditional language. First and foremost is the fact that the person is unable to spell-out (to hypercathect) the defence. This systematic absence of hypercathexis (and the limitations which it imposes on certain kinds of complex, abstract reasoning and prediction) constitute the 'blindness' or 'ignorance' in question. That this is a truncated ignorance is evident when we take into account the fact remarked upon earlier that patients in therapy report *remembering* that they did at some time in the past have certain aims or feelings which were then unconscious.

It may be appropriate to close these remarks with a few words on remembering what was unconscious. Memory is, after all, a chief source of un-deception in the eyes of not only Freud, but also Kierkegaard (and Camus). It seems to me that this remembering in the course of achieving insight can be taken in an almost straightforward sense, the single abnormality about it being that one was not able at the time to establish an attention hypercathexis of what one now hypercathects as a memory. We normally expect that the ability to spell-out something now as a memory is associated with the ability at the earlier time to spell it out as current engagement. But in the case of defence and subsequent insight, this expectation is not warranted. One cannot spell-out what one disavows (one cannot hypercathect what one counter-cathects). Yet this does not change the fact that an individual may be engaged in a certain way even though the person disavows it (the ego countercathects it). Once the engagement is avowed (the counter-cathexis is withdrawn), the capacity to spell it out now exists. But to spell-out the past as the past is what we term recalling. (Recollection is to memory as conscious is to preconscious.)

Thus it appears that the ability to spell-out at a certain time one's engagement at that time is not a necessary condition for recalling that engagement at a later time. Recollection of the unconscious is genuine recollection; it is not—as some have held, among them myself—the dawning and acceptance of a genuinely novel aperçu.

In seeing how recollection in therapy is authentic, we see that it is indeed not the essence of therapeutic progress, however characteristic it may be. It is alienation from or integration into the Ego which is fundamental to the therapy of defence.

CHAPTER SEVEN

THE AMBIGUITIES OF
SELF-DECEPTION—TO BE AND
NOT TO BE

THE move into self-deception is, as we know intuitively, a morally ambiguous move. So long as we take ignorance and knowledge to be central to self-deception, we can do nothing to resolve this ambiguity or to deepen our insight into it; we are left with the paradoxical truth that the self-deceiver 'in his heart' knows what he sincerely denies. This 'epistemological' paradox generates moral paradox since ignorance and blindness exculpate, whereas knowledge, insight and foresight inculpate. The inner structure of the moral paradox can now be laid bare if we abandon the 'cognition-perception' family of terms as central and make use of the analysis presented in preceding chapters.

Demos, in his original formulation of the problem of self-deception, holds that a critical moral attitude towards the self-deceiver is not only just, it is a criterion of our judging the person to be a genuine self-deceiver. The other philosophical analysts we discussed in Chapter Two do not concern themselves with this issue (and even Demos loses sight of it almost at once). Sartre and Kierkegaard, however, are most emphatic in their condemnation of the self-deceiver. On the other hand, Freud, as therapist, was the great exponent of the medical, non-judgmental attitude towards self-deception.

The contrast between the opposing attitudes is epitomized in the Sartrian attack upon Freud. Yet it is important to compare carefully Sartre's own doctrine of self-deception with his polemical presentation of Freud's. For the more one does so, the more one sees that what Sartre considers to be an intellectually unacceptable paradox when it is embedded in Freud's theory, he enshrines in his own doctrine as the ultimate postulate of a dialectical phenomenology of Consciousness. One might then suppose that Sartre merely prefers his dialectical language to Freud's physicalistic imagery. However there is more to it than that. It is, as we have noted, in their moral attitude to the self-deceiver that Sartre and Freud differ. Both conceive self-deception as essentially a kind of false consciousness, but Freud tries to account for this in the non-teleological language of defence 'mechanisms', mental 'systems', and 'energy' transfers, whereas Sartre tries to cast it in the insistently teleological language and imagery of choice, integrity, and responsibility. On the other hand, Freud never gets completely free of teleological language, though he claims this to be merely a short cut, a 'manner of speaking'; and Sartre, in delineating the ultimate, critical step into *mauvaise foi,* is forced in turn to reply upon a movement of consciousness in which it is the unwilled element which is crucial. Thus the attempts at total de-moralization or at total moralization of self-deception result, in each case, in taking in at the back door what was cast out from the front.

The analysis of self-deception as the disavowal of a

continuing engagement avoids the all-or-none approach, with its accompanying necessity for 'backdoor' manoeuvres. Let us see how this is so.

If we turn first to the context in which a person puts himself in self-deception, we can say, generally, that such a person has three options. We suppose, of course, that the individual is in a situation in which he is strongly inclined to a form of engagement which is radically inconsistent with the person's governing principles (the person's avowed aims, ideals, values, cultivated tastes, moral principles). One option under such circumstances is for the individual to forego the engagement, or to abandon it if he has already entered upon it in some degree. Normally, this is the chosen option of the adult person. To say that a person has put himself in self-deception, however, is to say that the person could not bring about a total abandonment of the engagement.

A second option is to pursue the engagement, the person avowing it as *his*. To do this would be for the person to face a spiritual crisis, for, to borrow the Kierkegaardian use of 'spirit' discussed earlier, the crises of spirit are the crises of the shaping, or the betraying, of the self. In the language of religion, it would be to confess one's finitude and, if the conflict is predominantly moral, one's sin; it would be to lay oneself open, vulnerable, as a radically divided nature, and to hope for the grace of some healing movement which it is not at the moment entirely within one's own personal powers to effect or even to foresee. Though we cannot know beforehand the outcome of such courage, the possibility of summoning it up must lie as a boundary, a spiritual horizon from which all self-deception must be viewed. From this perspective, self-deception is always a spiritual failure. Even from this perspective, however, we must recall how great the courage which may be required, how extreme the ordeal which may be involved, how genuinely devasting the outcome in which such an attempt may issue. It can be argued— as the Grand Inquisitor did—that the call of the perfect spirit is an impossible one for most of us. O'Neill's *The Iceman Cometh* is one of the great and humane contemporary sermons on the inhumanity wreaked by imperfect man when he attempts to adjure his 'pipe dreams' and accept himself as he is.

If there is a stalemate between inclinations which the individual will not give up, and the refusal by the person to avow these inclinations as his, there then remains one last option: the individual does engage himself in the way to which he is inclined, but the person refuses to acknowledge the engagement as his. This is man neither saved nor damned, in limbo, and at war with himself. It is from this perspective, so insistently favoured by Sartre and other Existentialists that we see how someone, by reason of lack of spiritual courage, attempts to save his integrity at a price which amounts to surrendering, however indirectly, the very integrity he cherishes.

We may note briefly that psychoanalysts characterize this same aspect of the movement into self-deception in terms of such morally neutral language as, e.g., 'the ego's capacity or incapacity to bear anxiety' and 'thresholds of excitation'. Nearer to the dramatic imagery favoured by theologians, moralists, and grand metaphysicians, but still clinically cool, is the Freudian formula, 'inner psychical conflict'.

Having paid due attention to the element of spiritual cowardice and inner warfare in the movement into self-deception, we must also appreciate that this cowardice and this warfare presuppose a person with a certain integrity. Not infrequently what is threatened is some aspect of integrity rooted in moral concern. The less integrity, the less is there motive to enter into self-deception. The greater the integrity of the person, and the more powerful the contrary individual inclinations, the greater is the temptation to self-deception (the nearer to saintliness, the more a powerful personality suffers). It is because the movement into self-deception is rooted in a concern for integrity of spirit that we temper our condemnation of the self-deceiver. We feel he is not a *mere* cheat. We are moved to a certain compassion in which there is awareness of the self-deceiver's authentic inner dignity as the motive of his self-betrayal.

It is this authenticity of moral concern rooted in personal integrity which constitutes the basis for optimism in using insight psychotherapy. The medically oriented psychotherapist is not likely to put matters this way, of course. He is more likely to speak of the patient's psychological maturity, or of the level of 'ego-strength' which is the necessary 'technical' requirement if insight therapy is to be indicated.

Having looked at self-deception 'judgmentally', both pro and con, we now turn to explore more fully the non-judgmental approach to self-deception, the view that the self-deceiver is not to be blamed, that he cannot help himself, that he is sick, or deceived (in a way). Rather than appearing as the *salaud* of Sartre or the double-minded sinner of Kierkegaard, the self-deceiver appears before us as the neurotic, as a victim of the compulsive force of the unconscious, as a sufferer from mental illness. To understand the force of this approach, we must turn our attention to another aspect of self-deception.

Disavowal is marked by (1) a surrender of that

special authority to express explicitly as one's own the engagement which is disavowed; (2) an authentic rejection of personal responsibility for the engagement and its consequences, rather than an irresponsible shirking of responsibility; (3) a certain undeflectable and irrational persistence in the pursuit of the dis-avowed engagement, this by virtue of its estrangement from that highly organized, evolving system of engage-ments which constitutes the person.

Taken as a group, these three features of disavowal strongly and rightly lead us to say, when there is disavowal, that in certain respects one does not have control over what one is doing. Furthermore, the inability to spell-out, because of its importance for sophisticated planning and assessment of complex engagements, leads to a profound further loss of self-control.

There is thus in self-deception a genuine subversion of personal agency and, for this reason in turn, a subversion of moral capacity. The sensitive and thoughtful observer, when viewing the matter this way, is inclined not to hold the self-deceiver responsible but to view him as a 'victim'. The more one concen-trates one's attention on these aspects of the matter, the less do condemnation and forgiveness seem relevant. Instead, the victim is to be pitied for the mental 'breakdown'. There emerges the 'medical' view of self-deception as helplessness due to 'mental patho-logy'.

The preceding remarks on aspects of self-deception provide a basis for insight into one of the most per-sistent controversies among psychotherapists. This is the question of the moral status of psychotherapy. There is a wide spectrum of views on this issue. At one end of the spectrum is such a view as Buber's, that psychotherapy is in effect a fully personal relationship aimed at spiritual and moral transformation. At the other end is the view, more or less held by many medical psychoanalysts, to the effect that psychotherapy is a 'technical', 'scientific', 'medical' procedure, having only 'health' as a value, and therefore being quite distinct from moral or religious preaching, teaching, or influence.

I have tried to show, in my earlier discussion of Freud, that he eventually appreciated that his therapy had always been oriented primarily to self-acceptance (removal of counter-cathexes) rather than to 'knowledge' (consciousness) as curative. Avowal of one's engagements is the optimal goal of classical psychoanalysis. Such avowal is the necessary condition of moral action, but is not itself moral action. It establishes the person as such in a particular respect and thus makes engagement in the moral life possible. As Freud said, the aim of psychoanalysis is not to tell the person what is good or bad, or right or wrong in a specific context, but to 'give the patient's ego freedom to decide one way or the other' (19, p. 50). The medical aim is thus in substance a spiritual aim. It is to help the individual become an agent and cease being a patient; it is to liberate, not indoctrinate.

When the Freudian emphasizes the compulsiveness of the unconscious, he is calling attention to the fact that it is indeed the individual who is acting, even though there is loss of direct control by the person; when the Freudian emphasizes the inner conflict between the 'forces' within different 'systems', he is pointing to the fact that the force of will is a critical factor, for the dilemma cannot be defined within, and therefore cannot be resolved within rational framework governing both 'systems'. The 'existentially' oriented psychotherapist raises similar issues with a different emphasis: he says that the world of the patient is through and through intelligible as the world of a human being, i.e., that it is a world of engagement, not the physicist's or the disinterested observer's world; and he says, further, that it is not by reference to established universal values but by a 'free', 'arbitrary', 'absurd' choice that the world of the patient will be of one kind or another. And, because the existentially oriented therapist adopts the emphasis he does, he prefers not to speak of a 'patient' at all.

If we turn for a moment from considering the role of therapists to a consideration of the role of moralist, ideologue, or minister, we can see now that insofar as they presume the self-deceiver to be fully a personal agent in the matter at hand, they preach, teach, and argue in vain. The futility of preaching to the neurotic has long been remarked by the psychiatrically oriented. Direct appeals to integrity and moral concern, by evoking the motives of self-deception, strengthen the inclination to it and are self-defeating.

What the self-deceiver specifically lacks is not concern or integrity but some combination of courage and a way of seeing how to approach his dilemma without probable disaster to himself. The nature of the help which the self-deceiver needs follows from this diagnosis. He needs someone who can help him, tactfully but persistently, through a detailed consideration of the texture of life. This helper must also offer evident, unswervingly dedicated reliability and dispassionateness, wide relevant knowledge, personal strength and humane tolerance; for the self-deceiver must be helped to go to the limits of his courage, but not provoked beyond the breaking point. This help is precisely what the ideal psychotherapist would offer. Of course there are no ideal therapists. And, on the other hand, there are others—preachers, teachers, friends, and relatives—who are likewise not ideal and who yet may demonstrate these qualities to some significant extent.

Most of the remarks I have made up to this point have been explicitly or tacitly concerned with 'classical' psychoanalysis, with the therapy of the person who is diagnosed as having a basically healthy ego, though suffering from relatively specific inner conflict. Yet not all mental pathology is of this kind, not even all the so-called psychogenic mental pathologies. I have said nothing directly concerning what psychiatry calls character disorders, psychoses, and other kinds of pathology rooted in severe ego and superego deficiencies. These types of psychopathology, along with obviously organically determined psychopathology, form the major part of the cases actually under psychiatric medical supervision. How does the account of self-deception that I have given apply in such cases? An early paradigm of psychotherapeutic treatment in one important class of such cases will be simple enough to summarize, and it reveals striking parallelism with my own theses. I will not attempt a comprehensive discussion of the gamut of psychopathologies.

In his work with young delinquents, the great August Aichorn found that for a certain large class of them, the first major therapeutic task is, paradoxically, to lead them to become neurotic. The young delinquents in question are those who frankly engage in behaviour which society forbids as immoral or illegal, and who do so not out of some deep commitment of their own, but irresponsibly.

The rationale for Aichorn's approach with such individuals was simple in its essence. Aichorn came to see them as persons who had not developed strong superegos; they had not 'internalized' parental and cultural moral demands. Thus appeals to conscience, to a concern for human values, were of course to no avail. To make the same point in the terms I used earlier (in Chapter Four), he found they had not learned the usual moralistic reactions associated with various forms of engagement; they had, inevitably, failed to develop adequately to the next level, the level of maturing as a person. Insofar as they had developed as immature persons, their major concern was with a complex of quite immediate gratifications rather than with deep attachments to other persons or to ideals.

Aichorn's therapeutic technique consisted in untiring attempts to establish a personal, parental relation, and as a consequence to evoke belated but essentially normal forms of engagement which included the guilt reaction. He argued on theoretical grounds, which he believed confirmed in practice, that with the emergence of a rudimentary superego (moralistic guilt reactions), the decisive condition for defence would be established. According to psychoanalytic doctrine, the intense moral anxiety evoked by a primitive superego as a consequence of its inflexible demands upon the ego is a typical condition of defence. This is particularly the case when the rigid prohibitions of the superego bear upon such powerful drives as those of puberty and adolescence, drives which the immature ego is quite unable to suppress or to sublimate. Unable to abandon a forbidden engagement, unable to avow the drives and bear the torment of a still immature and thus oppressive personal conscience, the person takes the last alternative, defence. This at least isolates the guilt-ridden project from the still immature personal self; it constitutes the first crude form of social and moral self-control which the juvenile delinquent achieves. But it is more than this. It is classical neurosis. It is the stage at which the therapist can proceed to more orthodox psychotherapy.

Now the therapist can gradually attempt two things. First, he tries to strengthen the young person's ego, i.e., to help him be courageous in the face of (moral) anxiety. Also, Aichorn tried to help the young person to learn how he could avow the impulse and the guilt, integrate them as part of the person and his conscience, transform and civilize them rather than being exhausted by warring with them. Once this therapeutic task was done, the youth was faced with the everyday tasks and problems of a person moved by conflicting aims. He could accept responsibility for himself and his deeds; he could assess his conduct morally according to his own moral vision.

Though the discussion in this chapter has concerned itself with the movement into and out of self-deception, we should not confuse this movement with movement into or out of moral responsibility. In practice, undeceiving oneself is typically associated with accepting responsibility. After all, the move *into* self-deception is motivated by a concern for personal integrity, and this typically is a concern for specifically moral integrity. We can therefore expect that with the acknowledgment by the person of his formerly disavowed engagement, that engagement will be taken up into the pattern of responsibilities accepted by the person. Nevertheless, if we are to have a large and clear view of the entire span of development here involved, we need to distinguish between avowal and acceptance of responsibility, between *personal* agency, and *moral* agency. The child of five or six years, for example, displays the marks of personal agency in many of his activities; he is clearly a *person* (unlike the one-year-old, who by and large is a creature of his environment and of the activities of the moment). Yet with regard to many of his personal engagements, the five-year-old is quite properly not yet held responsible. Though he is a person, he is not a responsible person.

I have argued at length elsewhere (*On Responsibility,* Ch. 2) that personal responsibility requires that the person tacitly or explicitly *accept* responsibility. Without that care and concern which express the acceptance of responsibility, the moral status of the person is akin to that of the minor who is able to act purposefully towards self-initiated ends, but who does not hold himself accountable and is not so held by others. Of course, in the case of the chronological adult who does not accept responsibility, the initially strong and generally reasonable tendency is for others to try to hold him accountable anyway. But, as I have argued in my systematic discussion of this problem, where there is genuine non-acceptance of responsibility, this attempt by others must in the end fail; it becomes vacuous in the face of authentic unconcern. (It is important to note that 'acceptance of responsibility', as I use the phrase here and in the cited work, refers to the person's concern or unconcern, not to his verbal protestations on the matter. Moreover, the issue is complicated by the fact that a person is responsible, in spite of unconcern with respect to a specific engagement, if there are other concerns of the person's by virtue of which he has indirectly committed himself to be concerned for the engagement at issue.)

This is not the place to re-argue the theses of my earlier study. It may suffice for the purpose of intelligibility, however, to repeat the point that this uncon-cern and absence of responsibility is found in a relatively pure form in the numerous instances of persons now usually classified in psychiatry under the rubric, 'sociopathic personality'. The ability to act intelligently but without any authentic moral concern is a chief characteristic of the sociopath. (It is the characteristic of the juvenile delinquents discussed earlier, though the treatable type of case discussed probably represents a simpler form of pathology than the most markedly sociopathic personalities exhibit.)

The sociopathic personality throws into sharp relief the distinction I wish to emphasize here. The distinction in question is that between the personal *identity* affirmation in avowal, the acknowledgment of an engagement as one's own personal engagement, and, on the other hand, acceptance of responsibility for one's engagements.

The person who does not display care and concern for his engagement, who does not accept responsibility for it, is the person most ready to avow such engagements (viz., the youth who admitted that he quite consciously abandoned his ageing, ailing mother alone in a car, since, as he readily also admitted, it made no real difference to him what happened to her). The person who cares deeply is, on the other hand, the one most tempted to disavow an engagement because of the burdens he not only foresees, but of his own free will would accept should he avow the engagement.

Thus avowal is a necessary condition of responsibility, and it is for this reason that disavowal expunges responsibility. On the other hand, it is because avowal is not a sufficient condition of responsibility that it is possible to become a person, achieve a personal identity (a rather limited identity, it is true) and yet be in significant degree non-responsible. This sequence has not been clearly noted before—it is consistently fused or blurred, as I have remarked earlier, by Existentialists. This is because, in practice, avowal is typically (but not necessarily) followed up by acceptance of responsibility for what is avowed.

I have referred to three characteristic ways in which avowal manifests itself: in assuming the authority to spell-out, in the integration of what is avowed into that achieved synthesis which is the personal self, and in accepting responsibility for the engagement avowed. As is now evident, these are not all necessary marks of avowal. In fact the first and second are essential manifestations of avowal, whereas a fair degree of acceptance of responsibility, though it is a very important and often readily noticeable mark of avowal, is usual but not necessary. We can add now that the degree to which the person is in general a responsible person determines, in general, the degree to which the person will accept responsibility for any particular avowed engagement. This is a corollary of the thesis that avowal is necessarily manifested by integration of the avowed engagement into the system of the personal self.

If I am correct in my proposals concerning the acceptance of responsibility, then we need to amplify earlier comments on the spiritual ideal of self-acceptance. We would now have to say, putting the matter quite generally, that the movement to becoming a responsible person has for its condition that the individual become a person, that although accepting oneself is the condition for accepting responsibility, the achievement of this condition is not a sufficient condition for becoming responsible. Though personal identity normally leads imperceptibly to a significant degree of personal responsibility, in some cases it hardly does so at all, and in general the achievement of each varies greatly among individuals.

We must now recognize that although self-acceptance is a spiritual ideal, it is not from the moral point of view a comprehensive or ultimate ideal, for moral responsibility must be a further fruition of self-acceptance. Yet this formulation raises further and profound questions which we are now in a position to approach, but which we cannot take up in a work whose principal aim has now been accomplished.

APPENDIX

THE NEUROPSYCHOLOGICAL
CONTEXT OF
SELF-DECEPTION

ONE of the main theses on which my argument has rested is that the skill of spelling-out is exercised with a certain decisive autonomy in relation to language use in general and our ability to engage in the world. Usually we do not distinguish the skill of linguistic expression so sharply; we tacitly view it as an integral aspect of the generic skill of using language. It was my analysis of consciousness and self-deception which led me to separate out this particular feature of language use as a quite special autonomous skill. The question to which I turn now is this: Is there any basis in neuropsychology for supposing that the expression in language of one's engagements could have a marked functional autonomy with respect to (a) other ways in which one uses language, and (b) the continuing of the engagement in question?

Certain aspects of recent neuropsychological research into brain structure and function warrant serious consideration in connection with such questions and, in general, with the problems examined in this book. Of course the conceptual and empirical problems posed

151

for neuropsychology are as yet vast. The principles which are appropriate to introducing neuropsychological data into our reflections here are (1) to seek to be as specific as possible concerning what we take to be the relevance of the neuropsychological data to the philosophical issues, (2) to identify and then to concentrate on neuropsychological fundamentals rather than on detail or on speculative, controversial refinements, and (3) in any case to consider the entire project as having value very largely for its suggestiveness rather than for decisive demonstration of a philosophical thesis.

The neuropsychological data and the philosophical investigations presented in this book were each developed entirely independently, both as a matter of history and logic. As will be seen, there is a remarkable coincidence of results between the two lines of investigation. In this Appendix, however, I shall merely try to paint in broad strokes, and with minimal technical paraphernalia, the relevant neuropsychological data. The interested reader is referred to the cited technical literature, to which my remarks are intended as an invitation and in no sense as a substitute.

It has long been held by neuropsychologists that, although the left and right hemispheres of the brain appear to be anatomically homologous, there are functional differences, one of these differences having to do with language. The left hemisphere of the brain has traditionally been called the 'dominant' or 'major' hemisphere, the right half the 'non-dominant' or 'minor' hemisphere. There has been a consistent preponderance of evidence that (1) the left (dominant) hemisphere is the one primarily associated with language, and, in addition, that (2) the left hemisphere primarily governs the right half of the body. Since most persons are 'right-handed', the left hemisphere may thus be thought of, broadly, as the 'dominant' one with respect to intellectual and motor functions.

The 'association' and 'governing' in question take their sense primarily from the following kind of evidence: damage to the left hemisphere is associated, far more dramatically and distinctively than damage to the right hemisphere, with pathology of language use or of motor use of the right side of the body. The precise nature and degree of the pathology depends to a significant extent on the region of the left hemisphere which is affected. Impressive correlations of specific regions of the brain with specific pathology have been made so far as a number of the functions, organs, and limbs are concerned.

Although the details which would fill out the preceding generalizations are very many, very complex, and often in controversy, and although the generalizations themselves are vastly in need of refinement and amplification, the main tenor of the generalizations is not controversial. A good deal of the evidence derives from relatively direct correlation of observable effects in body function or mental function as a result of the destruction or electrical stimulation of local areas of the cerebrum.

In the past half dozen years or so, a certain additional precision, of particular interest to us here, has been achieved in connection with a technique of cutting the great cerebral commissure (the corpus callosum). The great cerebral commissure is, roughly speaking, a broad cable of nerve material running along the midline of the cerebrum, between the two hemispheres. Its functions have until recently been most obscure. Mere severing of this commissure seemed to produce no significant difference in a person's (or animal's) subsequent performance on a variety of tests or as observed qualitatively in the clinic. This was a perplexing observation, since the corpus callosum, by virtue of its location, size, and internal structure, would seem *prima facie* to be very important for cerebral functioning.

During the past few years, however, new techniques for eliciting and discriminating laboratory performances of animals and human subjects have revealed that there are indeed remarkable differences in performance subsequent to severing the corpus callosum. These differences are due, it now at last appears, to the fact that severing the corpus callosum cuts direct intra-cerebral communication between the two hemispheres. This affords the opportunity, given sufficient experimental ingenuity, to assess the performance of each hemisphere independently of the other, and to draw inferences as to the role of intra-cerebral communication in the normal brain. No consequences from severing the corpus callosum had been noticeable to early observers because no attempt had been made to isolate the information coming to the brain so that it entered one hemisphere only. Hence both hemispheres could function on the basis of the same information, and on the basis of miscellaneous intra-bodily and other cues, and therefore the effects of cutting direct intra-cerebral communication were not readily observable.

Sperry, Gazzaniga, and others have demonstrated in the past decade and a half that the initiation of overt language use is peculiarly associated with the left hemisphere. The more general thesis that the left hemisphere governs language use was thus crucially refined. Both hemispheres are involved, in differing ways, in various forms of language and concept use. But *active* speech, the most noticeable to the observer, has a distinct anatomical, neurological, and functional autonomy in relation to other forms of language and concept use. The clinical details as revealed in the recent studies show striking similarities to distinctive features of self-deception, and of repression and defence. Let us explore the matter further.

After severance of the great cerebral commissure, it is possible to present visual or tactile information to the left hemisphere alone by providing the information to the right half of the visual field or to the right hand, respectively. Correspondingly, information is presented to the right hemisphere alone by providing it to the contralateral visual field or hand. (We shall not concern ourselves with experimental techniques here, ingenious and fascinating as some of these have been. The observations of human beings who have undergone commissurotomy has been possible because this surgical procedure is at times medically indicated for treatment of otherwise intractable epileptic seizures.)

Speech

In tests aimed to determine the capacity to speak with reference to information specifically lateralized to one or the other hemisphere, very different results were obtained for the right and left sides. Whereas spoken descriptions of stimulus material and other verbal responses obtained from the left hemisphere showed from the beginning little or no impairment, the right hemisphere appeared in similar testing to be totally incapable of speech.

. . . A familiar item placed in the subject's right hand, like a spoon, knife, comb, toothbrush, block letters, or any of a series of simple geometric shapes were readily recognized, named and described. . . . Speech was also used with normal facility in making various somatosensory discriminations involving weight, pattern, and temperature applied anywhere on the right half of the body. . . . In short, any sensory information entering the left hemisphere, or the results of the central processing of that information, could be reported through speech in much the usual manner.

Conversely, both subjects were totally unable to give accurate spoken reports for even the simplest kind of sensory information projected to the right hemisphere. . . . For example, a pencil placed in the left hand might go unnoticed and elicit no verbal comment whatever, or more typically, its presence would be recognized but it would be called a 'can opener' or a 'cigarette lighter', etc. Such guesses came presumably from the left dominant hemisphere and were based on whatever indirect cues happened to be available to that hemisphere. All visual stimuli flashed to the left half field similarly went undescribed or were reported vocally, as just a 'flash' or a 'white flash'.

Writing
The right hand with its main motor control centred in the left hemisphere along with speech was always capable of writing correctly the names and descriptions of visual or tactile stimuli presented to the left hemisphere with no special difficulty evident. When the same stimulus material was presented to the right hemisphere, however, none of the stimuli could be described or named in writing by any of the patients using either hand.

(Gazzaniga, 1967)

   In contrast to the above results, and in striking parallel to the theses of this book, are the experiments which show that the right hemisphere, though it cannot 'speak', can *understand* language and *act* intelligently on the basis of what it has understood. For example,

the examiner would read, 'Used to tell time', and would then flash five choice words in succession to the left visual field. In this instance the patients made a correct manual signal to the word, 'clock'.

Not only can the person understand language and respond skilfully, but he will show appropriate emotion. Thus, during a sequence of photos flashed to the left visual field, the subject blushes and smiles with embarrassment when unexpectedly a photo of a nude woman is presented. But in response to questions, the subject says she does not know why she is smiling, and didn't see anything. This may be observed in a film prepared by Professor Gazzaniga.)

The fact that the use of language for overt expression of one's perceptions, actions, feelings, etc., is functionally and neuroanatomically autonomous with respect to the use of language and concepts for other than overt expression makes much more plausible the thesis that spelling-out is a relatively autonomous skill. What we need to assume is that spelling-out is largely the same kind of activity as we have seen to be dominated by the left hemisphere in the commissurotomy experiments. Further, we need to assume that a similar functional divorce between an individual's engagement and his linguistic expression of that engagement need not require *physical* cutting of intra-cerebral communication but could be 'psychogenic'. The behavioural evidence concerning self-deception, and defence and the unconscious, strongly suggest that such communication can in fact be damped down, distorted, or cut off by 'psychological' means. This would be the neurological counterpart of what I have called disavowal and would be generated in disavowal. Investigations of the cerebral processes underlying such a psychogenic and highly specific 'commissurotomy' are, of course, outside the province of philosophical inquiry. But it is not beyond possibility that such reflections as the present ones can in turn suggest further lines of neuropsychological research.

The parallelism between my thesis and the neuro-psychological data becomes even more striking when we note that the subject receiving specific information only into the right hemisphere reacts to demands for spelling-out with other manoeuvres analogous to psychological defence: the left hemisphere 'searches' for some way to 'rationalize' the situation—by guesses, hunches, denials, rationalizations—and then expresses matters accordingly.

Let us recall the statement, cited earlier, that

. . . a pencil placed in the left hand might go unnoticed . . . or *more typically* its presence would be recognized (by the major hemisphere from intra-bodily kinesthetic cues) but it would be called a 'can opener' or a 'cigarette lighter', etc. (Italics and parenthetical comment added.)

Another typical example of the tendency to a rationalizing 'guess' by the left hemisphere may be noted in the following fuller version of an experimental report cited earlier. In this experiment, the subject hears the spoken phrase with both ears, and thus the spoken phrase of instruction registers in both hemispheres, but the correct response word is flashed only to the right hemisphere. Of particular interest here is the last sentence, omitted in the earlier citation:

For example, the examiner would read, 'Used to tell time', and would then flash five choice words in succession to the left visual field. In this instance the patients made a correct manual signal to the word 'clock'. When one of them was asked in passing what word he had seen, the reply (from the major hemisphere) was 'watch'.

The experiments are replete with instances in which the left hemisphere, deprived of direct information, proposes ingenious guesses or rationalizations which can be demonstrated to be dependent on specific, indirect clues, or to be quite unreliable.

As research workers in the field have noted, one inevitably begins to talk about the hemispheres independently, as if each were a separate individual. This way of seeing the matter is supported by a number of related experiments, e.g., the non-transferable learning which can go on in one hemisphere independently of, but concurrently with a different learning sequence going on in the other. In all this, the parallelism to our talk about the division of the psyche in defence and in self-deception is notable.

More generally, it should be noted that the left hemisphere is associated with the more intellectually elaborate performances of human beings. Calculation, and abstract reasoning of a high order seems generally to be rooted in left-hemisphere functions. Finally, and no doubt closely related to all the preceding, the left hemisphere seems to be dominant with respect to the co-ordination of projects which are themselves defined in complex and abstract intellectual terms rather than in fairly specific motor terms. All of this generally coincides with the thesis that the skill of spelling-out is, more than other forms of language and concept use, intimately associated with the self, the highest-order organization and unity of the individual human being. It also is reminiscent of the psychoanalytic postulate of a relatively autonomous mental 'system' organized in terms of 'secondary process'.

It is to be noted that, in general, the de-coordination of brain function as a result of brain damage—especially in the areas related to language use—has a range of effects remarkably suggestive, item for item, of the marks of the 'primary process' as Freud and others have described it. Among the early and typical signs of damage to the intellectual 'areas' of the brain are: drastic reduction of 'higher' rational powers (i.e., the powers of carrying on extended and highly abstract chains of reasoning), a tendency to move from one idea to another by virtue of memory associations, sound similarities, and visual similarities, a tendency to substitute parts for wholes, to ignore causal, temporal, and conceptual relationships. With all this, it must also be remembered that the intact right hemisphere, though incapable of verbal expression and generally limited in its intellectual capacities, does have at least the capacity for carrying out practical tasks involving relatively simple ideational, motor, perceptual, and emotional co-ordination. In short, there is ample neuropsychological basis for supposing that the carrying out of relatively simple human engagements is possible, though not with rational sophistication, without bringing to bear the capacities of the integrated 'self'.

What would be interesting, but what has not yet been done, is to feed a relatively elaborate and 'emotionally significant' project exclusively to the right hemisphere of the brain, to observe the consequent conduct, and at the same time to elicit regular 'reports' from the left hemisphere, as the latter picks up indirect cues, and totally invents where it must, in order to present a rational façade. Such a case might approximate more and more to the familiar features of self-deception, the ineradicable and no doubt important difference being that the entire affair would be 'artificially motivated' and rooted in physically induced commissural malfunction rather than in authentically motivated commissural misperformance.

Since I have distinguished, in Chapter Seven of the main text of this book, between the avowal of an engagement and the acceptance of responsibility for it, it may be worth noting that this distinction, too, has its analogue in the realms of neuropsychology. For some decades now the role of the frontal lobes of the brain has been studied, experimented upon, and, in gross terms, understood. The dramatic technique of pre-frontal lobotomy has accounted for much of the knowledge and the wide public acquaintance with the issues. Very briefly and roughly: the capacities for planning, for initiative, and for critical self-correction seem to be particularly associated with the frontal lobes. Thus an individual may have a reasonably clear inner sense of his personal identity and his engagements, and yet—with damage to the frontal lobes, or after lobotomy—he does not have the *concern* about himself or his engagements that he once did. He has less initiative in his affairs, or in set tasks; he is less rigorous and 'responsible' about carrying them out; he is less self-critical. The specific degree and character of the difference depends, of course, upon the specific nature of the lesion and of the person's character and circumstances. But the direction of change, after destruction of frontal lobe material, is unquestionable.

The anatomical and functional discreteness, as established in frontal lobe damage, of 'responsibility' inclinations on the one hand, and personal-identity, and linguistic-self-expression inclinations on the other hand, reduces the weight of any charge that the distinguishing of these types of inclinations at the level of moral psychology is *ad hoc*. What is more, considerations akin to those mentioned earlier in connection with spelling-out seem to apply here as well. They warrant the view that a *de*-coordination of personal identity responses and responsibility responses can be elicited by appropriate motives as well as by frontal lobe damage which leaves the speech centres unimpaired. I am not aware that anyone has yet explored the extent to which there might be pathology restricted to the frontal lobes in cases of severe and long-term sociopathic personality.

BIBLIOGRAPHY

1. ARLOW, J. A., and BRENNER, C., *Psychoanalytic Concepts and the Structural Theory,* International Universities Press, New York, 1964.
2. BULWER-LYTTON, EDWARD, *The Disowned,* in *The Complete Works,* 2 Vols., Thomas Y. Crowell & Co., N.Y., as date of publication.
3. CAMUS, A., *The Fall,* Vintage Books, New York, 1956.
4. CANFIELD, J. V., and GUSTAFSON, D. F., 'Self-Deception' in: *Analysis,* Vol. 23, 1962, 32-36.
5. DEMOS, RAPHAEL, 'Lying to Oneself', *Journal of Philosophy,* Vol. 57, 1960, 588-595.
6. EISSLER, K. R., 'On the Metapsychology of the Preconscious', in *Psychoanalytic Study of the Child,* Vol. 17, 9-41.
7. FINGARETTE, H., *The Self in Transformation,* Basic Books, Inc., New York, 1963 (Harper Torchbooks, New York, 1965).
8. FINGARETTE, H., *On Responsibility,* Basic Books, Inc., New York, 1967.
9. FREUD, SIGMUND, *The Standard Edition of the Complete Psychological Works,* The Hogarth Press, London, 1953-1966.
10. GESELL, A., and ILG, F. K., *Infant and Child in the Culture of Today,* Harper & Bros., New York, 1943.

11. GIDE, ANDRE, *Journal of The Counterfeiters*
     (Second Notebook); in *The Counterfeiters*, Modern
     Library, 1955.
12. GILL, MERTON M., *Topography and Systems in
     Psychoanalytic Theory*, Psychological Issues
     Monograph ♯10, International Universities Press,
     New York, 1963.
13. KIERKEGAARD, S., *Either/Or*, Vol. II, trans. W.
     Lowrie, Anchor Books, New York, 1959.
14. KIERKEGAARD, S., *Purity of Heart*, Harper & Bros.,
     Torchbooks, New York, 1956.
15. KIERKEGAARD, S., *The Sickness Unto Death*, trans.
     W. Lowrie, Anchor Books, New York, 1954.
16. MOLIERE, *Le Misanthrope*.
17. MURPHY, A. E., *The Theory of Practical Reason*,
     Open Court, Illinois, 1965.
18. NEMIAH, JOHN C., *Foundations of Psychopatho-
     logy*, Oxford University Press, New York, 1961.
19. O'NEILL, EUGENE, *The Iceman Cometh*, Random
     House, New York, 1940.
20. PENELHUM, T., 'Pleasure and Falsity', in *Philo-
     sophy of Mind*, ed., Stuart Hampshire, Harper
     & Row, New York, 1966, 242-266.
21. PEYRE, H., *Literature and Sincerity*, Yale Univer-
     sity Press, New Haven, 1963.
22. RIVIÈRE, JACQUES, *The Ideal Reader*, Meridian
     Books, New York, 1960.
23. RYLE, G., *The Concept of Mind*, Barnes & Noble,
     New York, 1949.
24. SARTRE, J-P., *Being and Nothingness*, trans. Hazel
     Barnes, Philosophical Library, New York, 1956.
25. SIEGLER, F. A., 'Demos on Lying to Oneself',
     Journal of Philosophy, Vol. 59, 1962, 469-475.
26. WHITE, A. R., *Attention*, Basil Blackwell, Oxford,
     1964.

SELECTED BIBLIOGRAPHY ON CEREBRAL COMMISSUROTOMY

1. BOGEN, J. E., and GAZZANIGA, M. S., 'Cerebral Commissurotomy in Man', *Journal of Neurosurgery, 23*, 1966, 394-399.

2. BOGEN, J. E., and VOGEL, PHILIP J., 'Cerebral Commissurotomy in Man', *Los Angeles Neurological Society Bulletin, 27*, 1962, 169-172.

3. GAZZANIGA, M. S., 'Cerebral Mechanisms Involved in Ipsilateral Eye-Hand Use in Split-Brain Monkeys', *Experimental Neurology, 10*, 1964, 148-155.

4. GAZZANIGA, M. S., BOGEN, J. E., and SPERRY, R. W., 'Laterality Effects in Somesthesis Following Cerebral Commissurotomy in Man', *Neuropsychologia, 1*, 1963, 209-215.

5. GAZZANIGA, M. S., and SPERRY, R. W., 'Language After Section of the Cerebral Commissures', *Brain, 90*, 1967, 131-148.

6. GAZZANIGA, M. S., BOGEN, J. E., and SPERRY, R. W., 'Observations on Visual Perception after Disconnexion of the Cerebral Hemisphere in Man', *Brain, 88*, 1965, 221-236.

7. PAILLARD, J., 'The Patterning of Skilled Movements', in *Handbook of Physiology*, Vol. III, Part I, 1960, Chap. LXVII, pp. 1679-1708.

8. PIERCY, M., HECAEN, H., and DE AJURIAGUERRA, J., 'Constructional Apraxia Associated with Uni-

lateral Cerebral Lesions—Left and Right Sided Cases Compared', *Brain, 83*, 1960, 225-242.

9. PIERCY, M., and SMYTH, V. O. G., 'Right Hemisphere Dominance for Certain Non-Verbal Intellectual Skills', *Brain, 85*, 1962, 775-790.

10. SPERRY, R. W., 'Cerebral Organization and Behavior', *Science, 133*, 1961, 1749-1757.

INDEX